CW00350838

As It Is Written

Interpreting the Bible with Boldness

by Benjamin Sargent

The Latimer Trust

As It Is Written: Interpreting the Bible with Boldness © Benjamin Sargent 2011

ISBN 978-1-906327-04-0

Cover photo © Silverpics – Fotolia.com

Published by the Latimer Trust December 2011

The Latimer Trust (formerly Latimer House, Oxford) is a conservative Evangelical research organisation within the Church of England, whose main aim is to promote the history and theology of Anglicanism as understood by those in the Reformed tradition. Interested readers are welcome to consult its website for further details of its many activities.

The Latimer Trust
London N14 4PS UK
Registered Charity: 1084337
Company Number: 4104465
Web: www.latimertrust.org
E-mail: administrator@latimertrust.org

Views expressed in works published by The Latimer Trust are those of the authors and do not necessarily represent the official position of The Latimer Trust.

Contents

1. Introduction

On what do we base our confidence that we can know and proclaim 'the message of Bible'? In a culture in which the Bible's message is challenged, contextualised, dismissed, or personalised, the claim that people should hear God's voice through the writers of preceding millennia can be disputed. This Study explores the philosophical integrity of such an assertion, and discusses the benefits and pitfalls of the various tools we might bring to the task of interpretation, drawing inspiration from Scripture's own methods as the Old Testament is applied in New Testament writings.

1.1. *Setting the scene*

The debate about how Christians ought to interpret the Bible is vibrant, vast and lucrative. In the last few years, Christian bookshops (especially those catering to an academic audience) have seemed near to overflowing with books on biblical interpretation. Many of these are concerned with recommending new and apparently exciting approaches to biblical interpretation, whilst some seek to introduce readers to the astonishing variety of interpretive options available to contemporary Christians, and others attempt to shore up the rapidly crumbling edifice of 'traditional' biblical scholarship. At the heart of this interest in theories of interpretation (or hermeneutics) is a scholarly malaise over historical criticism which dominated biblical scholarship throughout the 20th Century. Historical criticism, a way of interpreting Scripture exemplified by 19th Century German scholars such as Wilhelm M. L. de Wette and Julius Wellhausen, sought to provide a scientific approach to biblical interpretation, reading texts as historical artefacts best explained by reference to the historical situations in which and for which they were created. Historical criticism typically assumed that biblical texts could be most reliably explained without reference to God, indeed as features of a world in which God was not generally perceived to participate.[1] And therein lies the problem. With the advent of post-modernity with its stress on the legitimacy of all sorts of different views of the world, Christian biblical scholars have asked, quite rightly, why they are encouraged only to use an approach to interpreting the Bible which has no place in it for God. As a result, many are endeavouring to articulate alternatives to historical criticism and other methods which have been viewed as prejudiced against a Christian understanding of both the biblical text and the world itself. It ought to be noted that many scholars have employed historical criticism without compromising their Christian profession, yet such scholars represent a minority whose research is often dismissed by the historical-critical mainstream as 'conservative'. What has come to be recognised is that historical criticism is philosophically bankrupt: claiming an

---

[1] For example, as many who have studied the Bible using historical criticism will know well, it is typically assumed *apriori* that predictive prophecy (which represents just such a theological understanding of biblical literature) is an impossibility. This 'anti-theological' assumption has been used to date the Gospels in which the destruction of the temple is referred to and has stimulated significant discussion about possible referents of apparently predictive elements of the prophetic literature of the Old Testament. See, for example, W. C. Allen, *A Critical and Exegetical Commentary on the Gospel According to S. Matthew* (Edinburgh: T. & T. Clark. 1907), pp lxxxiv-lxxxv, W. G. Kümmel, *Introduction to the New Testament* (London: SCM. 1966), p 84, J. C. Fenton, *Saint Matthew* (London: SCM. 1973), p.11 and more cautiously, W. D. Davies and Dale C. Allison, *A Critical and Exegetical Commentary on the Gospel According to Saint Matthew, Vol I* (Edinburgh: T. & T. Clark. 1988), pp 131-132. Early works of 'historical criticism' famously took the accounts of miracles in the Gospels to task on the basis of similar assumptions about God's lack of involvement in the world, attempting to provide rational/ludicrous explanations of these events. See Albert Schweitzer, *The Quest of the Historical Jesus* (London: SCM.)

2

objectivity it could not possibly possess, claiming to speak universally though steeped in a single outdated worldview.[2]

This is definitely not a development which is of interest purely to academics, though. The discussion of how to interpret the Bible is something that has really assumed prominence following recent discussions relating to the place of practising homosexuals within the Churches' ordained ministries.[3] Indeed, many books of this genre specifically take up the issue of homosexuality. It is easy to see why so many new approaches to biblical interpretation have developed as a result of this debate. To most contemporary readers, whether Christian or not, the plain sense meaning of biblical texts like Romans 1:24 is 'homophobic'. If these contemporary readers are Christians who both want to continue to understand the Bible as inspired with a message of significant importance today and want to see barriers to the ordination of practising homosexuals removed,

---

[2] Nowhere is this better and more succinctly expressed than in Craig G. Bartholomew, 'Uncharted Waters: Philosophy, Theology and the Crisis in Biblical Interpretation,' in Craig G. Bartholomew, Colin Greene and Karl Möller (ed.) *Renewing Biblical Interpretation* (Grand Rapids/Carlisle: Zondervan/Paternoster. 2000), pp 1-34. See also Brevard S. Childs, *Introduction to the Old Testament as Scripture* (SCM: London. 1979), pp 39-40, Christopher Rowland, 'An Open Letter to Francis Watson on Text, Church and World,' *Scottish Journal of Theology* 48:4. 1995. p 511, Marcus Bockmuehl, 'Reason, Wisdom and the Implied Disciple of Scripture,' in *Reading Texts, Seeking Wisdom*, Ed. David E. Ford and Graham Stanton (London: SCM. 2003), pp 55-56, Alvin Plantinga, 'Two (or More) Kinds of Scripture Scholarship,' *Modern Theology* 14:2. 1998. p 250 and B. H. McLean, 'The Crisis of Historicism: And the Problem of Historical Meaning in New Testament Studies,' *The Heythrop Journal* (forthcoming: published online 2009).

[3] Cf. Oliver O' Donovan, *Church in Crisis: The Gay Controversy and the Anglican Communion* (Eugene, Oregon: Cascade Books. 2008), pp 54-68, Dale B. Martin, *Sex and the Single Savior: Gender and Sexuality in Biblical Interpretation* (Louisville: WJK Press. 2006), Stephen Fowl, *Engaging Scripture: A Model for Theological Interpretation* (Eugene, Oregon: Wipf and Stock. 1998), pp 119-126, Christopher Rowland and Jonathan Roberts, *The Bible for Sinners: Interpretation in the Present Time* (SPCK: London. 2008), pp 13-29 and Richard A. Burridge, *Imitating Jesus: An Inclusive Approach to New Testament Ethics* (Eerdmans: Grand Rapids. 2007).

then ways of reading the Bible which depart from an analysis of the 'plain sense' are encouraged.

1.2.   *What is at stake?*

And yet the issue of faithful biblical interpretation, if there is such a thing, far exceeds problems raised by ethical dilemmas such as homosexuality. Every act of biblical interpretation in the local Church can be called into question in ways which may never have been thought possible 20-30 years ago. Evangelical curates in their post-ordination training have provoked real anger when attempting to articulate a biblical view of a particular subject. 'How dare you presume to tell others what the Bible teaches? Let people rather be led to their own conclusions.' 'Surely Scripture is a gift from God – who are you to say what lessons I may learn from it?' One evangelical youth worker was recently rebuked by a vicar of a neighbouring parish for using the phrase 'the Bible says that...' during a school assembly. The vicar suggested that in future the phrase '*I believe* that the Bible says that...' ought to be used instead. It wasn't. The issue at stake here is whether or not we can be confident that what we proclaim from the Bible is more than our own opinion: whether or not there are good reasons for the interpretations we work hard at in the study, reasons which enable interpretations which are binding both on ourselves and on others. In other words, is there meaning in the Bible and can I be sure that I am teaching it faithfully? It is likely that as the variety of interpretive practice seen in the academic sphere trickles down to the local church, we whose responsibility it is to teach the word in season and out of season will be called upon more and more to give an account of why our interpretation is faithful.

And here we may be vulnerable as evangelicals who have a clearer sense than most on the nature of sound doctrine. Faithful interpretation is more than simply reading the Bible in such a way as to always come up with interpretations which agree with the doctrinal claims of classic Evangelicalism (though it is my belief that faithful interpretation will do this). It is all too tempting to assume that our interpretation is correct if we could imagine Calvin not being upset with what we preach. But as those familiar with the exegetical work of

Calvin will know, Calvin set less store by received doctrinal truth than he did by the fruits of prayerful attention to the details of the biblical text. If our interpretation of the Bible is justified to us simply by its agreement with received interpretation, we run the risk of becoming a self-contained tradition of interpretation which has little relevance to those outside it. My sermon this coming Sunday could then be described as 'an interpretation of Luke 16:19-31 in the evangelical tradition' rather than the proclamation of Luke 16:19-31 itself that I hope that it will be. We need to be able to justify our biblical interpretations to others without simply referring back to our own history of interpretation or the doctrines which others might already know that we believe but of which they are not persuaded.

1.3.   *Goals*

This Latimer Study aims to address some of the objections to the evangelical practice of preaching the 'plain sense' of biblical texts by exploring the nature of the earliest known Christian interpretation of Scripture seen in the use of the Old Testament in the New Testament. The interpretation of Old Testament texts offered in the New Testament is a good place to ground discussion of how Christians should interpret the Bible. For a start, it is at least clear that the New Testament writers did not seek to eradicate theology from their interpretation of texts, as was the case in historical criticism. Moreover, as I will note at various points, important features of the New Testament's interpretation of the Old Testament stand out from the practices common in and around the 1st Century AD, because of which such features deserve to be regarded as distinctively important for Christian interpretation of the Bible.[4]

---

[4]   At this point, it is worth noting that the discussion of New Testament use of the Old Testament in this study is primarily limited to discussion of formal citations: actual quotations which are subsequently commented on by the New Testament writer. This is not to ignore the vast significance of scriptural allusion in the New Testament. However, if one seeks to identify exegetical practice in the New Testament, it is much easier to do this by discussing formal citations where exegetical argument often comes to the fore.

With the aim of engaging with the challenges often posed to expository preaching from the contemporary interest in hermeneutical questions, this study will attempt to answer the following questions: 'Do texts mean anything?' In other words, is meaning a property of text, something that we can in fact discover and share with others? 'Do texts mean a single thing?' In other words, if texts do possess meaning, is there any point in seeking to distinguish between competing interpretations or do they all have something to offer? 'Does the text's author matter?' If one meaning is to be preferred over others, why should it be that intended by the author, if we can know what that might have been at all? And finally, 'Weren't things so different in those days?' Even if, for example, Paul thought such and such, what does that matter now – his cultural setting was so different to ours? In other words, is the historical difference between our situation and that of the text a stumbling block to receiving its plain sense meaning as the meaning for us today?

But before we look at these questions, it is worth briefly exploring the extent to which Christians today might employ the approaches to biblical interpretation seen in the New Testament. It is a major assumption of this study that to some extent the appropriation of some of these exegetical assumptions is helpful and indeed desirable. However, the issue of how Christians might learn from these has been debated at length, not least because of the sheer variety of approaches to interpreting the Old Testament which the New Testaments authors used.[5]

---

[5]   Major proponents of the view that contemporary biblical interpreters can, in some way, mirror the interpretive practices of the New Testament authors are G. K. Beale, 'Positive Answer to the Question Did Jesus and His Followers Preach the Right Doctrine from the Wrong Texts,' in G. K. Beale Ed., *The Right Doctrine from the Wrong Text? Essays on the Use of the Old Testament in the New* (Grand Rapids: Baker. 1994), pp 387-484 and Richard B. Hays, *The Conversion of the Imagination: Paul as Interpreter of Israel's Scripture* (Michigan: Eerdmans. 2005). For a more skeptical view see Steve Moyise, *Evoking Scripture: Seeing the Old Testament in the New* (London: T. & T. Clark. 2008).

1.4. Limitations

It is clear that to imitate some New Testament examples of scriptural interpretation would be to miss the point of why these examples are recorded at all. For example, Jesus' interpretation of Scripture in the Sermon on the Mount is significant not as an example of how we as Christians might interpret Scripture, but because of what it reveals about Jesus' own supreme authority to teach. Here, the response of the crowd is significant.

> And when it so happened that Jesus had completed these words, the crowd were amazed by his teaching for he taught as one who had authority and not as their scribes. (Matthew 7:28-29)[6]

Jesus' interpretation in this passage is understood to be unique. It is what is often termed 'charismatic exegesis': a type of interpretation which is utterly dependent upon the status and authority of the interpreter. For Christians, who understand Jesus' status and authority to be that of God incarnate who interprets Scripture as his own words, it is a mistake to copy this manner of interpretation because of its dependence on the unique status of Jesus as interpreter. Jesus' interpretation of Scripture in the Sermon on the Mount is striking precisely because it demonstrates an authority which is possessed by no-one else. Likewise, the Apostle Paul's interpretation of Scripture is dependent upon his apostolic authority which is described at the beginning of each of his letters.[7] At the same time, both Jesus and Paul often expound Scripture in a way that does not depend entirely upon their authority. In such cases reasons are

---

[6] This and all translations from the Bible in this publication are the author's own translations.

[7] However, the extent to which Paul can be regarded as exemplary for contemporary exegesis is fiercely contested. Richard Hays, for example, whom many would regard as the foremost authority on Paul's treatment of the Old Testament argues that contemporary Christians have much to learn from the way Paul interprets Scripture. See Richard Hays, *The Conversion of the Imagination*, pp 190-201.

given for the way in which a text is interpreted, reasons which make their interpretation transparent. Examples of this transparent or public type of interpretation include passages such as Matthew 22:41-46 and its synoptic parallels where Jesus teaches on Psalm 110:1 by asking a question about the text and thus urging his audience to understand its message. An example of this sort from Paul is found in Galatians 3:16 where Genesis 13:15 is interpreted as referring to one man, Jesus, on the basis that 'seed' is singular. Also worthy of particular mention is the treatment of Psalm 95:7-11 in Hebrews 3-4 where the author gives his readers three clear reasons to support his interpretation of that passage.

In other cases, where the authority of the interpreter is not stressed at all, this kind of public interpretation (interpretation performed, if you like, where everyone can see what is going on and how it has happened) can more easily be understood as providing an example to be imitated by others. Peter's sermon in Acts 2 provides a superb example of this which will be discussed in greater depth in subsequent chapters. Peter preaches under the power of the Holy Spirit who is promised as a gift to 'all who are far off, all whom the Lord our God calls' (Acts 2:39). There is no claim here to exclusive authority to interpret Scripture. Peter's interpretation of Psalm 16:8-11 here is utterly transparent. In verses 29-31, Peter lays out his case for interpreting the psalm as referring to Jesus using, firstly, a commonly accepted fact about David: that he died. The psalm which asserts that its speaker will not experience death and decay cannot possibly refer to its author David whose grave anyone can go and see.

Peter continues by building upon a lesser known idea[8] about David, that he was a prophet, from which he asserts that the psalm must be prophetic, referring forwards in time to Jesus who did triumph over death. Moreover, there is good reason to believe that this type of exegesis in Acts is already an imitation of an earlier example of public reasoning. Peter goes on in his Pentecost sermon to preach on Psalm 110:1 and again uses an understanding of David as its author to explain its meaning:

> David did not ascend into the heavens, but he said, 'the Lord said to my Lord, sit at my right hand until I set your enemies as a footstool for your feet.' (Acts 2:34-35)

Peter is not the first to take this (what is in 1st Century terms) unusual approach to Psalm 110:1. As was mentioned above, Jesus also approaches Psalm 110:1 in this way in Matthew 22:41-46.[9]

This modest discussion of a small selection of issues in contemporary biblical hermeneutics is offered in the hope that Christian readers will be encouraged faithfully to interpret the Scriptures with boldness: with conviction that there are good

---

[8] The exegetically important notion in Acts 2:30 that David ought to be understood as a prophet, whilst also present in *Tg. Ps* 49:16, is a clear feature of 11QPs³. In 11QPs³ 27:11 David's function as a prophet is used as a description of how the psalms were written, emphasizing their divine inspiration. Joseph Fitzmyer, 'David, "Being therefore a Prophet..."(Acts 2:30)', *CBQ* 34:3. 1972. p 337 suggests a possible relationship between what he sees as a qumranic tradition (seen partly in 11QPs³ 27:2-11, 1QM 11:7 and 6QD 3:4) that relates prophetic identity to the messiah. However, if this tradition is to have influenced the exegetical practice of the Pentecost speech, it seems most likely to have contributed to the interpretation of Psalm 16 which claims David as the Messiah, since the identity of David as the prophet and Jesus as the Christ are quite disconnected here. Peter W. Flint, 'The Prophet David at Qumran,' in *Biblical Interpretation at Qumran*, Ed. Matthias Henze (Michigan: Eerdmans 2005), pp 165-166 suggests that the idea that David was a prophet, seen in 11QPs³, may also have influenced 1QpPs, 4QpPs³ and 4QpPs^b.

[9] The historical relationship between these two discussions of Psalm 110:1 is discussed at length in my doctoral thesis.

theological and hermeneutical reasons for the interpretations they offer in the whole variety of Bible-teaching situations.[10]

---

[10] This study in no way seeks to cover the same ground already treated well in books such as Peter Adam, *Speaking God's Words: A Practical Theology of Preaching* (Leicester: IVP. 1996), Dale Ralph Davis, *The Word Became Fresh: How to Preach from Old Testament Narrative Texts* (Fearn: Mentor. 2006), Gordon D. Fee and Douglas Stuart, *How to Read the Bible for All Its Worth: A Guide to Understanding the Bible* (Grand Rapids: Zondervan. 1993) and Nigel Beynon and Andrew Sach, *Dig Deeper! Tools to Unearth the Bible's Treasure* (Leicester: IVP. 2005). These books provide practical advice on handling the Bible wisely and are to be commended. This study aims to explore some of the theory behind the Evangelical convictions about how the Bible should be interpreted which are promoted in books such as these. In particular, it seeks to defend them theologically with reference to the earliest Christian practice of scriptural interpretation: the use of the Old Testament in the New Testament.

2. Do texts mean anything?

We might take it for granted that texts mean things. When we write a letter we assume that it will communicate a particular meaning to the person who reads it. When we place a sign next our front door saying 'no junk mail, please' or 'we do not buy goods or services at the door', we assume that the sign is meaningful, though it rarely appears to be so. Texts seem to be meaningful, but a difficulty arises when we try to nail down how texts are meaningful. Is meaning a self-evident property contained within a text? If it is, how is it that intelligent and observant readers are able to come up with different interpretations of the same text? Why is it that the meaning of a well thought out text can often be ambiguous to certain readers? These questions seem to force the location of meaning into the realm of the reader: i.e. it is the reader who really provides the meaning of a text through his or her act of reading and interpreting it.

In a sense, the question of if and how texts mean things is foundational for every other area of discussion in hermeneutics. Certainly, subsequent chapters of this book, dealing with issues like whether or not there can be a variety of valid and even contrary interpretations of the same biblical text, are significantly affected by this initial question. If it is impossible to talk about textual meaning apart from the particular meanings of particular readers then there can be little doubt that there can be no privileging of one interpretation, or technique of interpretation, over others. So the discussion in this chapter is important, even if it may seem odd or unnecessary at first glance.

2.1. Inherent meaning in modern and contemporary philosophy

Twentieth Century philosophy was focused to a significant extent upon language and the interpretation of texts. This widespread interest has often been referred to as the linguistic turn in philosophy. Much of what has been said about language and the interpretation of written texts has undermined ideas about texts as inherently meaningful. Meaning of this sort has been questioned in a number of ways by a variety of thinkers. For existentialists such as Martin Heidegger, the 'meaning' of a text is entirely dependent on the present reality of the interpreter.[11] It is never something fixed and attached to the text, but is rather something which adapts to serve the reader in his or her quest for being or identity. For Julia Kristeva, who is largely responsible for giving scholars the term 'intertextuality' to describe how texts are formed from other texts, 'meaning' is never bound within a text since a text itself is usually a mishmash of other texts and ideas.[12] Texts constantly refer meaning beyond themselves to other ideas, other texts which themselves exist in a nexus of intertextual relationships. Jacques Derrida notes something similar in language itself which constantly refers or defers meaning beyond itself.[13] One word in a text only has meaning because of other absent words for which it stands in our minds. To interpret that word, readers need to consider others which in turn must be defined by yet others. For Derrida, language exists within an eternal chain of reference in which a text is simply an instance. A text can't, then, be explained on its own terms.

The existentialist emphasis upon the reader as the primary creator of meaning is seen in a more modest form in the work Paul Ricoeur, arguably the most prominent thinker in the field of hermeneutics of the 20th Century. Ricoeur notes that interpretation features consideration of a variety of 'worlds'.[14] An interpreter might consider the world-behind-the-text, exploring the possible historical

[11] Martin Heidegger, 'The Origin of the Work of Art,' in David Farrell Krell Ed., *Martin Heidegger: Basic Writings* (New York: Harper Collins. 2008).

[12] Julia Kristeva, *Desire in Language: A Semiotic Approach to Literature and Art.* (New York: Columbia University Press, 1980).

[13] Jacques Derrida, 'Cogito and the History of Madness,' in *Writing and Difference.* Trans. A. Bass. (London: Routledge. 1978), pp 36-76.

[14] Paul Ricoeur, *From Text to Action: Essays in Hermeneutics, II.* trans. Kathleen Blamey and John B. Thompson (Evanston, IL: Northwestern University Press. 1991), pp 87-88.

and authorial factors which make a text the way it is. He or she might consider the world-of-the-text, the reality which the text seems to present to the reader. However, readers can never escape the influence of the world-in-front-of-the-text: the present reality of the reader who decides the very questions asked of the text, who brings powerful and personal concerns to the text and who ultimately decides on the 'meaning' of the text. For Ricoeur, a text could never be regarded as inherently meaningful since reading can never take place without the influence of the world-in-front-of-the-text in which meaning is formed in relation to the concerns of the reader. Since such concerns differ between readers, 'meaning' likewise differs and cannot be regarded as an absolute property of the text. The role of the reader, or rather communities of readers, is extended beyond this in the pragmatic hermeneutics of Stanley Fish. For Fish, readers need to actively seek particular readings of texts, readings which benefit the community in which reading takes place.[15] Whilst Ricoeur encourages a dialogue between the various 'worlds' of the text, for Fish, only one 'world' is important: that of the reader. With pragmatic hermeneutics, one might regard meaning as utterly independent of a given text.

2.2. The rejection of inherent meaning by theologians

A theologian who shares something of this concern over the nature of textual meaning is A.K.M. Adam. Adam argues that those who approach the Bible as a document which contains meaning, uncritically accept a 'myth of subsistent meaning, the premise that

---

[15] Stanley Fish, *Is There A Text in This Class*, (Cambridge Mass: Harvard University Press. 1980), pp 147–174.

'"meaning" is a characteristic quality inherent in a text.'[16] He contends that there is simply no evidence that a text itself contains a single 'meaning' within it, a quality that the text itself is able to employ to govern interpretation, a quality that may protect the text from anarchic reading.[17] This is a criticism Dale B. Martin extends to the contemporary debate over homosexuality, pointing out how often biblical scholars claim that a text will not permit a certain interpretation due to certain feature of that text.[18] Martin suggests that this convention rests upon the same myth of subsistent meaning proclaimed by Adam. Hermeneutics used when approaching written texts are typically discussed in terms of their analogous relationship to various other forms of communication where meaning is intended in each act of communication and is usually understood by its intended target. Yet Adam argues that even commonplace non-written acts of verbal and non-verbal communication are without inherent meaning; a subtle hint made to a neighbour, an eye full of tears: these by no means communicate a single unambiguous meaning.[19] Why should one assume that written texts do? Adam's point is that so many acts of communication are ambiguous. In the light of this ambiguity it seems absurd to suggest that meaning subsists in acts of communication necessarily. It is worth remembering that some communication which appears ambiguous is deliberately so, in which case ambiguity might be conceived of as an

---

[16] A. K. M. Adam, *Faithful Interpretation: Reading the Bible in a Postmodern World* (Fortress: Minneapolis. 2006), p 2. Cf. Fowl, *Engaging Scripture*, pp.33-34. Adam, along with many others, also helpfully questions the philosophical assumptions of historical-criticism and their relation to Christian Theology. This is particularly the case in his essay, 'Docetism, Käsemann, and Christology: Why Historical Criticism Can't Protect Christological Orthodoxy,' *SJT* 49:4. 1996. pp.391-410, which questions the assumed neutrality of historical criticism and the theological benefit which is supposed to proceed from this.

[17] Adam, *Faithful Interpretation.*, pp 2-4.

[18] Martin, *Sex and the Single Savior*, p 1.

[19] Adam, *Faithful Interpretation*, pp 6-7. Cf. A. K. M. Adam, 'Poaching on Zion: Biblical Theology as Signifying Practice,' in *Reading Scripture with the Church: Toward a Hermeneutic for Theological Interpretation* (Baker: Grand Rapids. 2006), p 27.

element of meaning. One thinks of contemporary liturgy of the Church of England which attempts to appeal to a variety of theological sympathies, or poetry which is written with the intention of provoking a variety of impressions when performed. Even Adam's own example of the subtle hint to a neighbour aims to do two things at once: giving instruction whilst trying to avoid the impression of giving instruction, opening up the real possibility that the hint is received in entirely the wrong way. Adam is ultimately interested in furnishing Christians with an hermeneutic through which to read Scripture. His criticism of 'subsistent meaning' is not a theological critique, though. Instead, it proceeds from a set of observations about ordinary language. This is worth commenting on at this stage.

2.3.   General or special hermeneutics?

Hermeneutics is often divided into two broad groups: general and special. General hermeneutics is concerned with the interpretation of any kind of text or work of art and involves discussion of widely applicable interpretive strategies. Special hermeneutics is much more focussed and often assumes that certain types of text require interpretive strategies of their own. For example, the interpretation of poetry requires the reader to understand that poetic language may well be figurative, whilst the interpretation of a Biology text-book will not require this.

One of the biggest debates in biblical interpretation in the last two or three centuries has been whether the Bible ought to be interpreted according to general hermeneutical theory (i.e. interpreted like any other book). Prior to the reformation, with possible exceptions such as the 'Antiochan School', the Bible was interpreted with its own special exegetical rules. Most notably, the activity of biblical interpretation was carried out by a limited clerical group, with a yet more limited range of interpretive outcomes open to them. Whilst the reformation introduced to biblical interpretation methods of interpretation that had previously been used primarily on classical literature, biblical interpretation was still primarily performed as a special hermeneutical domain. For example, the Bible was still regarded as 'Scripture': as literature with unique and compelling status and authority, and was read as a single body of literature imposing a need to appreciate its teaching as a whole.[20] The movement towards biblical criticism, itself a development of the reformation's hermeneutical emphases beginning with Benedict de Spinoza in the 17th Century, represents the first concerted attempt to read the Bible like any other book. Spinoza wanted Scripture to be studied using the 'scientific' methods one would use to understand anything else in the world.[21] And this aim is reflected in Benjamin Jowett's much later contribution to *Essays and Reviews* which caused

---

[20] This principle is seen clearly in the XXXIX Articles of the Church of England. Article XX: '...it is not lawful for the Church to ordain anything that is contrary to God's Word written, neither may it so expound one place of Scripture, that it be repugnant to another.' It can also be seen in article VII: 'The Old Testament is not contrary to the New: for both in the Old and New Testament everlasting life is offered to Mankind by Christ, who is the only mediator between God and Man, being both God and Man.'

[21] Benedict de Spinoza, *Theological-Political Treatise*, trans. Michael Silverthorne and Jonathan Israel (Cambridge: Cambridge University Press. 2007), p 98 '...I hold that the method of interpreting Scripture, does not differ from the [correct] method of interpreting nature, but rather is wholly consonant with it. The [correct] method of interpreting nature consists above all in constructing a natural history, from which we derive the definitions of natural things, as from certain data. Likewise, to interpret Scripture, we need to assemble a genuine history of it and to deduce the thinking of the Bible's authors by valid inferences from this history, as from certain data and principles.' This principle of constructing the 'true' history behind the biblical text dominated early historical criticism and can be seen very clearly in Julius Wellhausen, *Prolegomena zur Geschichte Israels* (Berlin. 1885) who sought to shed light on the Old Testament by formulating an 'objective' and 'scientific' account of the history of Israel the manner described by Spinoza. Indeed, John Milbank, Theology and Social Theory: Beyond Secular Reason, 2nd Ed. (Oxford: Blackwell. 2006), p 20 lays the blame for historical criticism's prejudice against Christian doctrine with Spinoza. According to Milbank, Spinoza developed the nominalist distinction between the phenomenal and the noumenal to the point at which any sense of God's participation in the ordinary processes of his creation, such as the writing of texts, was rendered impossible.

a storm in 19th Century Britain.[22] The recent movement toward theological interpretation of the Bible represents an attempt to make biblical hermeneutics 'special' again, partly in response to the demise of modernity with which the historical criticism of Jowett was associated.

However, despite the recent trend towards recovering special biblical hermeneutics, general hermeneutical theory has a great deal to offer to the discussion of whether texts possess meaning as a sort of quality inherent within them. Hans-Georg Gadamer, a seminal figure in 20th Century hermeneutics, likened reading texts (or rather, engaging with works of art generally) to being involved in a game.[23] The game, or rather the act of playing itself, acts upon the player so that as he plays he can't dismiss it as meaningless. Strikingly, given the context of the discussion of this chapter, Gadamer speaks of the ontology of texts, suggesting that texts have deep, even *meaningful* inherent qualities: that they are more than a collection of signs on a page.

> If, in connection with the experience of art, we speak of play, this refers neither to the attitude nor even to the state of mind of the creator or of those enjoying the work of art, nor to the freedom of a subjectivity expressed in play, but to the mode of being of the work of art itself....What is play is not serious. Play has its own relation to what is serious...It is more important that play itself contains its own, even sacred, seriousness...The player himself knows that play is only play

---

22 Benjamin Jowett, 'On the Interpretation of Scripture,' in *Essays and Reviews* (London: Longman, Green & Co.. 1869). Jowett famously argued that Christian doctrine ought to be set to one side when the Bible was read. Perhaps ironically, this way of reading is derived from the reformation principle of *sola scriptura* which encourages Christians to let the Bible speak for itself without the stifling and misleading direction of the (Roman) Church.

23 The idea of textual agency, the understanding particularly of the Bible as something with active qualities, is something I explore in greater depth in Benjamin Sargent, 'The dead letter? Psalm 119 and the spirituality of the Bible in the local church', *Evangelical Quarterly* 81:2. 2009.

and exists in a world which is determined by the seriousness of purposes. But he does not know this in such a way that, as a player, he actually intends this relation to seriousness. Play achieves its purpose only if the player loses himself in his play. It is not that relation to seriousness which directs us away from play, but only seriousness in playing which makes play wholly play. One who doesn't take the game seriously is a spoilsport. The mode of being of play does not allow the player to behave towards it as if it were an object.'[24]

Interestingly, Gadamer discusses the ontology of the text as something experienced in and through the text itself, without reference to its 'creator'. Texts are simply experienced as meaningful, as affecting those who engage with them, just as a game becomes 'serious' and real as it is played. In this way the meaning of a text is something experienced as real, as the text acts upon its reader. Perhaps this is what is meant in the phrase, 'the Scripture moveth us in sundry places to acknowledge and confess our manifold sins and wickedness,' from morning and evening prayer in the Book of Common Prayer. Did Cranmer conceive of Scripture as something active, something that drives us towards a conclusion and an action we could not have arrived at ourselves? That when we read the Bible it actively does something to us? This is certainly what is meant in Hebrews 4:12-13, where God's living and active word is described as seeking out and disclosing the hidden places of our hearts.

But, going back to Gadamer, just because texts *can* be experienced as meaningful, does that mean that they are inherently, as a feature of their ontology? Neither the Bible nor the Prayer Book seem to go so far as to suggest this. Can't texts also be experienced as meaningless, just as a game can often seem confusing and fail to

Moral level?

---

[24] Hans-Georg Gadamer, *Truth and Method*, trans. William Glen-Doepel (London: Sheed and Ward. 1975), pp 91-92. Something similar can be seen in Roland Barthes' description of the 'text of pleasure' and the 'text of bliss', both of which *act* upon the reader, in Roland Barthes, *The Pleasure of the Text*, trans. Richard Miller (New York: Noonday Press. 1975) p 14.

grasp its players with a sense of its reality? So what, then, of Adam's critique of the idea that the Bible is inherently meaningful? Is he right? The fact is that a text taken in complete isolation is almost meaningless. Texts are normally interpreted within a context which gives them meaning. This is certainly the case regarding Gadamer's use of the ontology of play – the text only becomes 'real' when it is entered into, i.e. which it is given a context, a relationship to its reader. This is certainly true, too, in everyday life. When someone receives a letter a process of establishing the letter's context begins. Firstly the enveloped is examined. Is this addressed to me? Is the name right? Is it spelled correctly? What does the type of envelope tell me about the letter inside? Does the envelope suggest who it's from? Once opened, was anything else (e.g. a free pen) included inside? Is it typed or handwritten? Is it written in blood or using cut-up letters from a magazine?! What does the letter head say? Who is it from? All these questions are asked before the letter itself is read. The answers construct a sense of the context in which the letter is interpreted. Without this contextual information we would be unlikely to begin reading the letter. A sentence saying 'meet me at the station at the usual time' means nothing without information about whom it is from and whom it is for, from which knowledge about this context supplies the details of the exact station, time and the reason for meeting. Similarly, the sentence 'it has come to our attention that you have paid insufficient tax for the financial year 2009-2010' begs the question, 'who does "our" refer to?' without which it cannot be reliably interpreted. Does it refer to a group of people seeking to blackmail you, a group of lone sharks sensing an opportunity, a tax fraud company or HM Revenue and Customs? The answer to this question makes a significant difference to how the sentence is read and therefore the meaning which it has for the reader to whom it is addressed.

Texts have meaning when they are placed within a framework which enables them to be understood as discourse: as an act of communication.[25] It is not as though they have meaning independent of the communicative act which they serve. This assumption that texts must be understood as someone's attempt at communication with ourselves or with someone else comes naturally to us. It is certainly something that appears to be universally assumed within biblical preaching. This is seen in the widespread association of biblical texts with personal names – John, Luke, Jesus, Paul etc. – the personal names of those who communicate through the text. At the same time, biblical texts are given a context in preaching insofar as they are read as being directed at us: they address us and our needs now. These two ways of giving a text the kind of context in which it can have meaning are very much a part of how New Testament authors interpret Old Testament texts too. Scripture is always seen as bearing some relation to an author in the past, readers or significant events in the present, or both.

2.4.   Text contextualised as discourse in the New Testament

This tendency to 'contextualise' Scripture in the New Testament is widespread and could possibly be demonstrated for each citation of, or allusion to, the Old Testament in the New Testament. One clear example is the use of Scripture in Romans 14:7-12. Here Paul offers a closing charge to his mixed Jewish and Gentile readers, urging them to accept one another. He supports his charge with a series of biblical citations; 2 Samuel 22:50, Psalm 18:49, Deuteronomy 32:43,

---

[25]   Hence another influence of 20th Century general hermeneutics upon biblical interpretation is John L. Austin's 'Speech Act Theory.' This influence can be seen particularly in Nicholas Wolterstorff, 'The Promise of Speech-Act Theory for Biblical Interpretation,' in After Pentecost: Language and Biblical Interpretation, Ed., Craig Bartholomew, Colin Greene and Karl Möller (Zondervan/Paternoster: Grand Rapids/Carlisle. 2002), idem., Divine Discourse: Philosophical Reflections on the Claim that God Speaks (Cambridge: Cambridge University Press. 1995), Kevin J. Vanhoozer, First Theology: God, Scripture and Hermeneutics (IVP: Downers Grove. 2002) and idem., 'From Speech Acts to Scripture Acts: The Covenant of Discourse and the Discourse of Covenant,' in After Pentecost: Language and Biblical Interpretation, Ed., Craig Bartholomew, Colin Greene and Karl Möller (Zondervan/Paternoster: Grand Rapids/Carlisle. 2002).

Psalm 117:1 and Isaiah 11:10, all of which feature the common term (*Stichwört*) 'Gentiles'. These texts, which each indicate something of God's hope for the salvation of Gentiles, are meaningful to Paul's audience because the audience is seen to stand at the point in salvation history when this hope is coming to pass. In other words, these texts which Paul offers are either understood as being about his audience (in the case of the Gentiles) or directly addressing the real concerns of his audience (in the case of the Jewish believers, trying to understand how to relate to Gentile believers). Likewise, in Acts 4:25-26, Psalm 2:1-2 is related to specific events of significance to the Jerusalem church.

The view of New Testament authors that Christian believers share in the story of Israel and therefore find Scripture addressed to them is expressed most clearly in the discussion of Psalm 95 in Hebrews 3-4, an example of biblical interpretation which will be returned to in subsequent chapters. Psalm 95, clearly understood as written by David in a different time and place from the audience of Hebrews (Hebrews 4:7-8), is seen nevertheless to address them directly. Psalm 95 is understood to be spoken by David to God's people of the past, yet at the same time it is spoken by the Holy Spirit to God's people of the present, 'today', in Hebrews 3:7. Yet it is the same message which is held out in each context: the promise of entry into God's rest. This message to God's people is addressed directly to those of the past just as it is to those of the present (Hebrews 3:6,14). Psalm 95 is God's direct discourse to his people through time. It has meaning for God's people in the first Century A.D. because they are part of the people of God to whom Scripture is God's speech. And, the author of Hebrews would tell us, Scripture is addressed to us in the 21st Century too if we hold firmly to our faith in Christ.

Even Hebrews 2:6, which introduces an Old Testament quotation in the most impressively elusive manner in the New Testament, places its quotation within a relationship to contemporary readers which gives it meaning. Hebrews 2:6 introduces a quotation from Psalm 8 with the words 'someone has testified somewhere...' Yet, even here, a piece of Scripture which the author of Hebrews appears to know little about has astonishing power to tell the audience of Hebrews something it doesn't know about the Lord Jesus. Because Psalm 8 is understood to be about Jesus and because of the author of Hebrews' perception that βραχύ ('little') refers to a short period, rather than a definition of status, this enables readers to identify with the psalm's account of Jesus' yet-to-be-completed glorification, and the psalm has real meaning. Because Scripture here speaks of the Church's Lord, it has meaning for the Church. Because Scripture here tells the story of Jesus' glorification of which Christian readers are a part, it has meaning for Christians. Incidentally, this may be a means of understanding why we need God's help to interpret his word faithfully, since it is as the people of God, caught up in the plan of God, that it has meaning for us.

Whilst it may be a challenge to describe all texts as meaningful, especially as 'possessing' meaning, Christians should be able to interpret the Bible as a meaningful document. Whilst the Bible can (and perhaps should) appear strange and difficult at times to Christians, it always has meaning because it tells a story of which Christians in any century are a part. In a sense, it is about us because it is about the God whose people we are, made possible through the story of rescue it tells. The Bible becomes meaningful, then, when it is given a context: when it is seen as dealing with things of value to us as Christians and the world to which we hold out the word of truth. This is most definitely a special 'theological' approach to meaning. There is, in a sense, no access to this meaning for those who are not part of God's covenant people. But for Christians, biblical texts are more than a mere jumble of meaningless words. Meaning can be sought with boldness.

3. Do texts mean a single thing?[26]

It is quite popular in contemporary Christianity to assume that if
biblical texts are meaningful and communicative then they must be
open to a variety of valid interpretations. This is often expressed most
strongly in some forms of Evangelicalism, where a high view of
biblical inspiration leads to a sense that the finite text of Scripture
cannot limit the communicative possibilities open to the Holy Spirit.
In some ways, this belief has had a very positive impact on the use of
the Bible in local churches. The belief in polysemy (that the text is
open to a variety of interpretations) empowers ordinary Christians to
read and interpret the Bible with the expectation that they will hear
God's voice. Belief in polysemy means that Christians don't need
experts to tell them what the Bible says.

Yet polysemy also raises significant dangers. If a text can
mean a variety of different (and perhaps even contradictory) things,
its authority is dissolved except in what it might be thought to say to
an individual. Though this was never the case in the medieval uses of
polysemy, in which interpretation was often tightly policed, in the
contemporary context the belief makes interpretation personal and
private with little relevance to others. Whenever biblical study is a
feature of one of the diocesan study days I am from time to time
required to attend, the typical question asked is 'what is this passage
saying to you?' Why 'to you?' The assumption is that a particular
passage will mean different things to different people. This makes
any sense of proclaiming Scripture to others deeply problematic.
When polysemy is assumed by a congregation, biblical preaching will
always be perceived as simply an interpretation: one particular

---

[26] An earlier attempt of mine to grapple with this issue can be found in Benjamin
Sargent, 'One Meaning or Many? A Study in New Testament Interpretation of
Old Testament Texts,' *Churchman* 124:4. 2010. This chapter will attempt to add
to what I discuss there, particularly in terms of its concentration on the use of the
Old Testament in 1 Peter.

understanding of a given passage. Polysemy robs any form of biblical teaching of its power. Those who hear biblical preaching as simply *an* interpretation; one of many possible interpretations, are more likely to dismiss hard teachings which confront them and demand repentance, teachings which are perceived as the pastor-teacher's own thoughts. In short, polysemy enables a pick-and-choose approach to allowing the Holy Spirit to do his work through the teaching of his word. Because of this, it can completely undermine the high view of Scripture's authority on which it so often depends.

Another side-effect of the belief that Scripture is polysemous is a lazy approach to teaching the Bible. I once heard someone training for full-time pastoral ministry express how much he enjoyed leading small group Bible studies. They were so easy to lead, he said, because they required little preparation. After all, he said, there are no right or wrong answers when it comes to studying the Bible. In his case, a laudable belief in biblical inspiration and a confident trust in the Holy Spirit to be at work in the small group led him to disregard the value of preparation. This is a real danger, because as those who regularly lead small groups know all too well, many understandings of the Bible aired in small groups are far from constructive.

3.1. *Theologians who assert polysemy*

Despite the apparently problematic nature of polysemy, it is embraced enthusiastically by many theologians interested in biblical interpretation.[27] For example, Stephen Fowl says regarding determinacy (the view that a text has a single meaning) that,

> Determinate biblical interpretation seeks to secure stability
> and coherence for Christian faith, worship, and practice, by

---

[27] Often the rejection of the notion that texts have a single meaning has been part of a much broader rejection of historical criticism. Certainly, a defence of single meaning (determinacy) has been a feature of the broader defence of historical criticism. See John Barton, *The Nature of Biblical Criticism* (Louisville: Westminster John Knox. 2008), pp 160-161.

ascribing a particular, stable and coherent property to the Bible (i.e. meaning). Following the proper interpretive procedures for extracting meaning will be a necessary first step. This view, however, is theoretically mistaken in thinking of meanings as properties of texts, and theologically mistaken in locating the bases of coherent and faithful Christian faith and practice in the text of the Bible, interpreted in isolation from Christian doctrines and ecclesial practices.[28]

For Fowl, determinacy is implausible because it requires a belief in meaning as an inherent property of the text, as discussed in the previous chapter. He also suggests that a rigorous and methodical quest for a single meaning of a biblical text is likely to take biblical interpretation away from addressing the needs of the community in which it is interpreted. This need not be the case, though. In fact, one of the clearest early examples of determinate biblical interpretation is that of the Dead Sea Scrolls. Here the needs of the community drive exegesis towards a single goal, based on the assumption that Scripture relates primarily to the events of which the community is a part. Fowl's contention is that vigorous interpretation which aims to define a single meaning can only be abstract and academic, divorced from real life situations. Biblical interpretation at Qumran proves that this is not the case as the community understood Scripture to have a single meaning and yet interpreted it as being about their particular situation.

But for others, the very fact that the Qumran community of the Dead Sea Scrolls and others have insisted on the single meaning of Scripture is evidence that Scripture is necessarily polysemous. If many different groups claim to teach the single meaning of Scripture, either a great number of them are wrong or perhaps there are different 'literal' meanings for different communities and so Scripture is really polysemous. This has been argued by Hans Frei and Christopher Seitz who note that 'literal' meaning is, more than anything else, the meaning which appeals the most to a particular

---

[28]   Fowl, *Engaging Scripture*, p 40.

community or interpreter, rather than a single meaning bound to the text itself.[29] One can certainly imagine that a community for which a certain idea, such as 'covenant', is particularly important will see covenant in every verse of the Bible, even when it would be utterly unconvincing to anyone without that obsession. But, whilst biblical interpretation is always at risk from being governed by the interests of its readers, there are certain ways of reading Scripture which allow it to speak with a voice different to our own. These will be explored in the next chapter.

Perhaps the most serious objection to determinacy is the claim that it is simply not Christian. Rowan Williams argues against determinacy by suggesting that the literal sense of Scripture has not been understood in Christian theology as determinate, but rather is something which constantly changes as Christians engage with the text through the changes of time.[30] For David C. Steinmetz, determinacy represents an Enlightenment rejection of the polysemy of traditional 'pre-critical' biblical interpretation, in particular, the various levels of meaning in medieval exegesis.[31] Steinmetz suggests that determinacy is more a feature of historical criticism, with its prejudice against theological interpretation, than it is of Christian approaches to the Bible. This is a serious criticism. If determinacy is only possible by rejecting or limiting the divine inspiration of Scripture and thus its theological potency, surely Christians ought to think again about whether the meaning of Scripture is determinate? But is it really just a novel and anti-theological imposition on biblical interpretation? James D. G. Dunn notes that, for example, John

---

[29] Hans W. Frei, 'The "Literal Reading" of Biblical Narrative in the Christian Tradition: Does it Stretch or Will it Break?' in *The Bible and the Narrative Tradition*, Ed. Frank McConnell (Oxford: Oxford University Press. 1986), pp 37-61 and Christopher R. Seitz, *Word Without End: The Old Testament as Abiding Theological Witness* (Eerdmans: Grand Rapids. 1998), p 12.
[30] Rowan Williams, 'The Literal Sense of Scripture,' *Modern Theology* 7:2. 1991. p 123.
[31] David C. Steinmetz, 'The Superiority of Pre-Critical Exegesis,' in *The Theological Interpretation of Scripture: Classic and Contemporary Readings*, Ed. Stephen E. Fowl (Oxford: Blackwell. 1997), pp 26-38.

Colet's 1496 lectures on the Bible at the University of Oxford place considerable stress on the single literal sense of Scripture.[32] Likewise, and perhaps more significantly, Scripture is treated as determinate according to its literal sense in the political writings of William of Ockham.[33] Ockham's writings on the power and nature of the state, as well as on papal authority, apply Scripture in an uncomplicated literal manner, as a clear source of information and prohibition. Perhaps most significantly, though, determinacy appears to be a significant feature of the way New Testament authors understood the interpretation of the Old Testament.

3.2. Determinacy in 1 Peter

Elsewhere I have written a brief overview of scriptural determinacy in the New Testament.[34] Rather than repeat the various discussions of a wide range of biblical writers and their apparent approaches to plurality in interpretation, in this chapter discussion of the New Testament's use of the Old Testament will focus on the use of Scripture in 1 Peter. 1 Peter has much to commend itself to those wanting to understand Scriptural interpretation in the New Testament. It contains a significant number of clear citations of Scripture,[35] citations which play important roles in Peter's arguments. Peter's use of Scripture is intricate. He refers back to citations after they have been quoted. He uses language and imagery associated with citations, or from their immediate literary context in the Old

---

[32] James D. G. Dunn, 'Criteria for a Wise Reading of a Biblical Text', in *Reading Texts, Seeking Wisdom*, Ed. David F. Ford and Graham Stanton (London: SCM. 2003), p 42.
[33] This is seen most clearly in Ockham's *Dialogus.*
[34] Sargent, 'One Meaning or Many?'
[35] It is, of course, notoriously difficult to identify quotations in the New Testament, some of which may be only a few words long and a possible coincidence, such as ὡς λέων ὠρυόμενος in 1 Peter 8:5, a possible citation from Psalm 22:14. There are probably about 20 quotations and many more allusions in 1 Peter: a significant number for such a short book, suggests W. L. Schutter, *Hermeneutic and Composition in 1 Peter* (Tübingen: Mohr-Siebeck. 1989), p 3.

Testament, when interpreting them. Moreover, 1 Peter (though perhaps less than 2 Peter) discusses the nature of Old Testament prophecy in 1:10-12 and also displays a significant theology of God's word in relation to Isaiah 40:6-8. 1 Peter is also interesting because, unlike other New Testament books, there is little consistency in citation formulae used to introduce passages from the Old Testament.[36]

Before any citation from Scripture appears in his letter, Peter offers an account of how Scripture was written and what it refers to. He tells his readers that the prophets of the past wrote Scripture through the 'Spirit of Christ'. They sought the meaning of their words earnestly and found that they referred to the things of the Gospel proclaimed to the Church.

> About this salvation, the prophets who prophesied the grace which is for you, searched carefully, carefully seeking for which[37] time and circumstance the Spirit of Christ testified to beforehand: the Christ's sufferings and the glory after. It was revealed to them that they were serving not themselves but us who have now had announced to us – through those who have proclaimed the Gospel by the Holy Spirit sent from heaven – that which angels long to see. (1 Peter 1:10-12)

In a sense, this is Peter's biblical hermeneutic.[38] Scripture's meaning is related to one particular set of events: 'the Christ's sufferings and

---

[36] However, Peter frequently uses the words διότι and γάρ, whilst using the more conventional formula διότι γέγραπται ὅτι once.

[37] Cf. G. D. Kilpatrick, '1 Peter 1:11: TINA 'H ΠΟΙΟΝ ΚΑΙΡΟΝ,' *Novum Testamentum* 28:1. 1986. pp 91-92.

[38] For example, J. Ramsey Michaels, *1 Peter* (Nashville: Thomas Nelson. 1988), p.175 explains that it is because of Peter's view that the prophets were 'Christians before the coming of Christ' that he is able to interpret Psalm 34:12-16 the way he does in 1 Peter 3:8-12. However, it must be noted that Edward Gordon Selwyn, *The First Epistle of St. Peter: The Greek Text with Introduction, Notes and Essays* (London: MacMillan. 1958), pp 133-134 takes 'prophets' in 1:10 to refer to Christian, rather than Old Testament, Prophets. Whilst this view is certainly plausible, there is nothing particularly in the text to commend it above other

the glory after.' The prophetic authors themselves <u>found their own</u> <u>words perplexing</u>: they didn't seem to have an <u>obvious referent</u> in <u>their own time</u> but pointed forward to a <u>yet inexperienced reality</u>. For Peter, the meaning of Scripture is limited. Rather than meaning a variety of things through time, <u>Scripture refers to one reality alone.</u> Scripture, whilst written in the past, yearns towards a single 'certain time and circumstance' (singular) in which it finds its meaning. Apart from this single referent, the prophets experienced their Spirit-of-Christ-inspired utterances and writings as lacking meaning. Hence they sought it earnestly. 1 Peter 1:10-12 provides a clear statement of scriptural determinacy, emphasising the single meaning of scriptural texts. This is particularly noticed here by Pheme Perkins who finds determinacy deeply problematic:

> The difficulty that this section of 1 Peter poses for Christians today lies in its appropriation of the Old Testament. The letter never suggests [ie. mentions] that there is another community of Jewish readers for whom the prophets do not describe Jesus...No doubt persons who had grown up as members of the Qumran sect might say the same about the prophets and

---

interpretations. Indeed, the repeated use of aorist verbs in 1:10-12 seems to mediate against a sense that such prophecy is ongoing. Cf. J. N. D. Kelly, *A Commentary on the Epistles of Peter and Jude* (London: A. & C. Black. 1969), pp 59 and 61-62 and Paul J. Achtemeier, *1 Peter* (Minneapolis: Fortress. 1996), p 108. It is rather unfortunate that D. A. Carson, '1 Peter,' in G. K. Beale and D. A. Carson (Ed.), *Commentary on the New Testament use of the Old Testament* (Grand Rapids/Nottingham: Baker/Apollos. 2007), pp 1015-1045 does not discuss 1 Peter 1:10-12, probably because it contains neither citation nor allusion. In a sense, this passage parallels the similar reflection in 2 Peter 1:19-21. In 2 Peter, the prophetic word is said to be 'made more certain/ made firm' for the followers of Jesus to whom Peter writes. Kelly, *Peter and Jude*, p 321 says that 'the true meaning, which the Greek construction fully supports...is that in the light of [the transfiguration of Jesus] the message of prophecy has been made 'more sure' in the sense that God has Himself certified it as true and that it is already in the process of fulfillment.' For a contrasting view, see Richard J. Bauckham, *Jude, 2 Peter* (Nashville: Thomas Nelson. 1983), p 223. Bauckham notes that when Thucydides uses this phrase it lacks the legal sense of confirmation. He therefore translates the clause as 'we place very firm reliance on the prophetic word'.

their [own] origins.[39]

For Perkins, Peter's assumption that Scripture refers only to Christ is arrogant because it ignores the many Jewish people who read those same Scriptures without seeing Christ in them. Yet the notion that the Scriptures find their true meaning in Jesus Christ and his kingdom governs the use of the Old Testament in 1 Peter. This happens in two ways: Firstly, the Scriptures are seen to define the identity of Jesus and his followers to whom they refer exclusively as prophecy and promise. Secondly, the Scriptures are used to provide moral exhortation in a manner which is specific, though probably universally applicable to God's people through time.

A good example of this first use of Scripture can be seen in 1 Peter 1:22-25. Isaiah 40:6-8 is seen to refer directly to the 'word that was preached to you' (v 25), which, one can deduce from the similar expression in 1 Peter 1:12, is the Gospel of Jesus Christ. Isaiah 40:6-8 is seen to refer directly to the Gospel and the community of those who will be born through that imperishable word.[40] This is a real case of the prophet looking forward to the things of Christ and his Church. As is often the case in the New Testament, a quotation from Scripture is applied directly and simply to the Christian situation in a manner which appears unequivocal: 'this is that' as F. F. Bruce characterises

---

[39]   Pheme Perkins, *First and Second Peter, James, and Jude* (Louisville: John Knox Press. 1995), p 35.

[40]   The sense in which the use of Isaiah 40 supports the determinacy of Scripture suggested in 1:10-12 is enhanced by Steve Moyise, 'Isaiah in 1 Peter,' in Steve Moyise and Maarten J. J. Menken Ed., *Isaiah in the New Testament* (London: T. & T. Clark. 2005), p 177. Moyise argues that the substitution of 'Lord' for the Septuagintal 'God' in the quotation was designed to enhance the Christological value of the text in line with Peter's view of the Old Testament. However, it is notoriously difficult to identify when or if New Testament authors change the wording of Old Testament quotations since, as R. T. McLay, *The Use of the Septuagint in New Testament Research* (Michigan: Eerdmans. 2003), p 6 points out, Greek Old Testament textual traditions are unlikely to have been as fixed in the first Century as is suggested by the idea of the Septuagint. See also, R. A. Kraft, 'Para-mania: Beside, Before and Beyond Bible Studies,' *Journal of Biblical Literature* 126:1. 2007. pp 11-17.

the practice.[41] In terms of the discussion of determinacy, this is interesting because the New Testament authors appear to rule out other interpretations when they read Scripture in this way: they appear to understand scriptural texts as having a single referent. Likewise, in 1 Peter chapter 2, three Old Testament quotations[42] united by the common word, 'stone' are interpreted as referring to Jesus and those destined to respond incorrectly to his message. This is another example in which the reality to which Scripture is seen to point is that laid out in 1:11-12 – nothing other than the ministry of the Christ and the new covenant people he would bring into being. In the same way, and perhaps for obvious reasons, Isaiah 53 is interpreted as referring to the death of Jesus.

Scripture is not only seen as predictive, the work of prophets who looked forward to a single coming era, it is also exhortative, speaking words of rebuke and encouragement directly to Peter's audience. Psalm 34 is employed in just this sense in 1 Peter 3:8-12.[43] Peter's audience is exhorted to be sympathetic to their brothers and sisters in the Church, showing love, offering blessing and rejecting evil. This exhortation is supported by the citation from Psalm 34:12-16 which encourages much of the same in the form of a promise. Likewise, the exhortation to be holy in 1 Peter 1:14-16 is supported by a citation of the repeated exhortation to be holy from Leviticus. Peter's view of Scripture's determinate meaning is seen here in the way in which his exhortations stem from a clear assumption that Scripture unambiguously exhorts God's people to the same things: 'do this, because it says in Scripture that you should do this!' There is no sense in these passages that the scriptural quotation directly *describes* the early Christian situation. However, Scripture is seen to speak directly to the needs of Peter's

---

[41] F. F. Bruce, *This is That: The New Testament Development of Some Old Testament Themes* (Exeter: Paternoster. 1968), pp 19-21.

[42] Isaiah 28:16, Psalm 118:22 and Isaiah 8:14.

[43] Sue Woan, 'The Psalms in 1 Peter,' in Steve Moyise and Maarten J. J. Menken Ed., *The Psalms in the New Testament* (London: T. & T. Clark. 2004), pp 222-223 notes the straightforwardly moral use of this psalm, both in its citation as well as in allusions to it in 2:1-3.

audience. It would be wrong to read into 1 Peter a salvation-historical framework through which this direct discourse becomes possible, in which followers of Jesus are seen as the continuation of the people of God to whom the scriptural text was originally intended.[44] Despite this, when Scripture is cited as providing some sort of clear imperative or exhortation a single and unambiguous meaning is assumed. Here the citation formulae are significant. Whilst it is disputed by Paul J. Achtemeier, it seems likely that Peter introduces texts as proof texts, texts whose meaning is assumed to be obvious to his audience.[45] These proof texts require no explanation as to how they are being used since their single meaning is assumed. This is also the case in Paul's similar use of Scripture, often introduced with proof-text-type formulae.[46] Indeed, if one looks outside 1 Peter, evidence for early Christian belief in Scripture's determinate meaning is all over the New Testament. Luke writes of Scripture fulfilled uniquely and exclusively for all time in and through the Lord Jesus.[47] In Hebrews chapters 3-4, Psalm 95:7-11 is seen to refer to one thing alone: the eternal promise of rest which remains for followers of Jesus, whilst in Hebrews chapter 1, a whole host of Old Testament texts are cited as unambiguous proofs of the Son's status. For Paul, Scripture is not only the clear proof of Gospel about Jesus, it is also something which can only be understood in the light of the Gospel.[48]

---

[44]   John H. Elliot, *1 Peter: A New Translation with Introduction and Commentary* (New York: Doubleday. 2000), p 17 argues, however, concerning the use of the Old Testament in 1 Peter that 'linking the eschatological community with the history of God's covenant people, this material served to stress the social estrangement and oppression of God's people as resident aliens in diaspora.' Cf. John H. Elliot, *A Home for the Homeless: A Sociological Exegesis of 1 Peter, its Situation and Strategy* (London: SCM.1982), pp 183-184, for example. However, there seems to be little evidence that Peter understood the scriptural texts he cites to refer in some prior sense to Israel. Yet there is a clear sense of salvation history in 1:10-12, as the prophets look forward to the day of Christ and his people and, also in 3:5-6 in which the 'holy wives' of Israel's history are seen as examples to Christian women, suggesting some sense of historical continuity.

[45]   Achtemeier, *1 Peter*, pp 12-13.

[46]   Elliot, *1 Peter*, p 18 appropriately notes a similarity with Qumran in this respect too.

[47]   See Luke 1:4, 54-55, 4:18-22, 24:27, 44, Acts 2:25-31, 3:17 and 13:27 for example.

[48]   Sargent, 'One Meaning or Many?' p 362.

This insistence on Scripture's single meaning is all the more astonishing when one considers that the rabbinic exegetical literature with which the New Testament is often compared generally emphasises polysemy.[49] Far from being anti-Christian, a mere product of Enlightenment historical criticism, determinacy appears to have a significant Christian pedigree. Christians with a responsibility for teaching the Bible should not shy away from working hard at identifying and proclaiming the single meaning of Scripture: the unambiguous voice of God to teach, rebuke, correct and train in righteousness.[50] For it is only when Scripture is heard as coming from God, not being the mere interpretation of a human being, that the man of God will be equipped for every good work.

---

[49] It could be argued that an appropriate emphasis upon both authorial intention and the single meaning of a biblical text is undermined by the typological reading of the Old Testament in the New Testament. Does typological reading of the Old Testament provide another, different meaning in addition to the historically intended 'plain-sense' meaning? Does this suggest that a different approach to interpreting the Old Testament is needed to allow contemporary Christians to add typological interpretation in a way they may not when interpreting the New Testament? It is perhaps wrong to regard a typological interpretation as providing an additional meaning to a passage. Typology grows and develops out of a literal understanding of a character in the Old Testament who is then explored in relation to the bigger story of which he or she is a part. As biblical authors understood themselves to be writing as part of a yet unfolding drama of God's salvation, they themselves would not intend the characters or events they describe to be read in isolation from this narrative. Typological reading is an extension of meaning, rather than a creation of new meaning. And there is nothing to stop the New Testament from being read typologically – indeed it may be part of the author's intention for it to be read in this way. For example, one might read the good Samaritan as a type of Christ. The good Samaritan assists a man who hates him and pays his debt. He fulfills the righteous requirement of the law which the teacher of the law knows he cannot fulfill and hence knows that he does not have what it takes to obtain eternal life. Indeed, Jesus tells this story to demonstrate what law fulfillment looks like. And again, this is an extension of meaning using Luke's own theology of who Christ is and why he has come: it is not something which goes beyond Luke's intention.

[50] 2 Timothy 3:16

4. Does the text's author matter?

If texts are meaningful vehicles for communication, if they are attempts to convey a limited and specific meaning, how should one go about ensuring that such meaning is received through interpretation, rather than some other spurious meaning? Looking back to the earlier illustration of receiving a letter, it must be said that ordinarily we interpret texts by placing them within a particular set of contexts. The little note which says 'meet me at the station at the usual time' begs the immediate question, 'who is this from?' If this text cannot be imagined as belonging to a particular individual about whom something is known, it is meaningless. As an act of communication, this note fails if it is not clear from whom it comes. So, in our day to day written communication, authorship is very important. We do not send letters without including within them a clear sense of who we are. Often the claims or recommendations we make in written communication are only possible because of the sense of who we are as authors. A GP writing to a patient giving advice about treatment needs to make her identity absolutely clear through headed paper, an address, a signature and correct knowledge about the patient if her letter is to be successful. If the reader does not see the relationship between the GP and the letter he might dismiss the advice as the interference of some unqualified busybody.

Every day, as we are presented with a whole variety of texts, we make judgements about those texts and what they mean by thinking about authorship. But is this the same with the Bible? Do some texts 'mean' things independently of their authors? Does it matter what a biblical author intended to communicate when writing under the inspiration of the Holy Spirit?

It may be fair to say that, generally, Christian readers of the Bible have not thought the identity of biblical authors to be of much interpretative significance, apart from establishing the canonical authority of particular texts.[51] So why, then, should we consider authorial intention to be important?

4.1. The pedigree of authorial intention

Many theologians and philosophers associate authorial intention exclusively with the aims and presuppositions of Enlightenment historical criticism.[52] Because of this, it is often rejected along with the whole historical-critical project as something riddled with post-Enlightenment prejudice against theology. It is certainly true that the quest for authorial intention was a significant element in historical criticism. But can that quest be understood independently from Enlightenment prejudice?

John Barton and Joseph Fitzmyer, two leading biblical scholars, have recently written defences of historical criticism against contemporary accusations, such as that mentioned above. Common to each defence is an attempt to demonstrate that the interests of historical criticism are pre-modern, thereby proving that they cannot be dismissed with the Enlightenment. Fitzmyer argues that historical criticism has its roots in the 'text-critical' work of the Alexandrian grammarians of the 3rd and 2nd Centuries B.C..[53] He then sees the use of Alexandrian methods of interpretation in the Patristic era, particularly in Origen's *Hexapla* (his parallel-text edition of the Greek Bible, commonly known as the Septuagint) and works by Augustine

---

[51]   The very long standing discussion of the authorship of Hebrews is a case in point. Whilst contemporary discussion has little bearing on issues of the text's theological authority, earlier work had a significant impact on how the text was received by Christians. See Clare K. Rothschild, *Hebrews as Pseudepigraphon: The History and Significance of the Pauline Attribution of Hebrews* (Tübingen: Mohr Siebeck. 2009).

[52]   For example, Rowan Williams, 'Historical Criticism and Sacred Text,' in *Reading Texts, Seeking Wisdom*, Ed. David E. Ford and Graham Stanton (London: SCM. 2003), p.221 and Paul Ricoeur, *Hermeneutics and the Human Sciences*, Trans. J. B. Thompson (Cambridge: Cambridge University Press. 1981), p 201.

[53]   Joseph A. Fitzmyer, *The Interpretation of Scripture: In Defense of the Historical-Critical Method* (New Jersey: Paulist Press. 2008), p 61.

and Jerome. Barton's history of biblical criticism does not go back quite so far as Fitzmyer's, concentrating on renaissance humanism, both Catholic and Protestant.[54]

However, there also appears to be some degree of interest in using ideas about authorship to explain Old Testament texts in the New Testament. If this is the case, it really cannot be argued that interest in authorial intention is anti-theological and dependent upon the Enlightenment. The purpose of this chapter is to demonstrate that authorial intention is not simply a product of the Enlightenment. It is a feature of some of the use of the Old Testament in the New Testament. It is certainly not a feature of all use of the Old Testament in the New, indeed, much of this interpretation does not demonstrate any interest in a human author. What is important, though, is for us to understand authorial intention as a genuinely theological interest, one which deserves a special place within contemporary biblical hermeneutics after the Enlightenment.

The argument in Acts 2:29-35 is a good example in the New Testament of an Old Testament text being interpreted in the light of its author. The Apostle Peter's interpretation of Psalm 16:8-11 begins just after it has been cited.

> Men brothers, let me say with confidence to you about the patriarch David that he reached the end of his life and was buried and his tomb is with us to this day. But David, being a prophet and seeing that God had sworn on oath that he would sit the fruit of his loins upon his throne, foresaw and spoke about the resurrection of the Christ that he would not be 'abandoned to Hades' nor would his flesh 'see corruption.' God has raised this Jesus, of which we all are witnesses. Therefore he has been exalted to the right hand of God and has received the promised Holy Spirit from the Father and has poured out this which you see and hear. For David did not ascend to the heavens, but he said 'the Lord said to my Lord:

---

[54]   Barton, *Biblical Criticism*, pp 124-132.

"Sit at my right until I set your enemies as a footstool for your feet.'"

Peter demonstrates two types of author-based reasoning. Firstly, in a negative sense, Peter uses the facts of David's own death to work out that neither Psalm 16 nor Psalm 110 can be about their author: they cannot be self-referential. David was not preserved from Hades and corruption, nor did he ascend to the heavens.[55] That is as factual as the presence of David's tomb. Secondly, in a much more positive manner, Peter defines David's identity in order to understand what kind of referent Psalm 16 might have. Since David was a prophet, so Peter argues, he was likely to have been writing about some time in the future.[56] In first Century terms, this second argument is unusual and quite sophisticated. The text discussed by Peter is seen to find its meaning once the identity of its author has been asserted. Prophet David would mean his psalm to be prophetic. The closest comparison with this type of argument in ancient literature is indeed the Homeric scholarship of the Alexandrian Grammarian, to which Fitzmyer

---

[55] Jacob Jervell, *Die Apostelgeschichte* (Göttingen: Vanderhoeck & Ruprecht. 1998), p 147. 'Eine solche „negative" Verwendung von David kommt im Neuen Testament nur bei Lukas vor. Die Psalmstelle kann nicht von David handeln, den er sah Verwesung: er starb und wurde begraben, wurde auch nicht von den Toten auferweckt, denn man kann noch heute sein Grab „in unserer Mitte" sehen. Sien Tod ist unbestreitbar.' Cf. Mark L. Strauss, *The Davidic Messiah in Luke-Acts: The Promise and its Fulfillment in Lukan Christology* (Sheffield: Sheffield Academic Press. 1995), p 138, Hans Conzelmann, *Acts of the Apostles: A Commentary on the Acts of the Apostles* (Philadelphia: Fortress. 1987), p 21, Gregory V. Trull, 'Peter's Interpretation of Psalm 16:8-11 in Acts 2:25-32,' *Bibiotheca Sacra* 161. 2004. p 440, Ben Witherington, *The Acts of the Apostles: A Socio-Rhetorical Commentary* (Eerdmans: Grand Rapids. 1998), p 146. and on Ps 110:1 specifically, Jürgen Roloff, *Die Apostelgeschichte* (Vandenhoeck & Ruprecht: Göttingen and Zurich. 1981), p 60. 'David ist nicht zum Himmel aufgefahren, er kann also die Aussage seines Psalms, die von der Erhöhung des „Herrn" spricht, nicht im Blick auf sich selbst gemacht haben. Deren wahre Bedeutung enthüllt sich also vom Weg Jesu her.'

[56] Joseph Fitzmyer, 'David, "Being therefore a Prophet..."(Acts 2:30)', *Catholic Biblical Quarterly* 34:3. 1972. p 332 notes that it is David's identity as a prophet that enables him to refer to the future in Psalm 16.

refers as a possible source for the historical-critical tradition. Grammarians like Aristarchus of Samothrace based many of their exegetical and textual decisions upon a developed understanding of who Homer was, as the poetic author of the works they studied.[57]

---

[57] Aristarchus did this by creating a clear view of Homer as φιλότεχνος (Filotechnos), as the perfect literary craftsman. This can be seen in Scholia A on *Il.* 2.681a. Yet this notion is by no means a novel invention of Aristarchus'. Gregory Nagy, 'Early Greek Views of Poets and Poetry,' in *The Cambridge History of Literary Criticism, Vol I: Classical Criticism*, Ed. George A. Kennedy (CUP: Cambridge. 1989), p 19 notes that τέχνων was a common early metaphor for the work of the poet, seen for example, in Pindar Pythian 3.113. Despite the use of a term like φιλότεχνος, Aristarchus never elaborates a theory of poetics (though this does not mean that he did not have one). Cf. James I. Porter, 'Hermeneutical Lines and Circles: Aristarchus and Crates on the Exegesis of Homer' in *Homer's Ancient Readers: The Hermeneutics of Greek Epic's Earliest Exegetes*, Robert Lamberton and John J. Keaney (ed.) (PUP: Princeton. 1992) pp 71-72). The use of this term, however, illustrates his understanding of Homer as the 'serious, perfect craftsman' who is unlikely to be inconsistent. Dirk M. Schenkeveld, 'Aristarchus and ΟΜΗΡΟΣ ΦΙΛΟΤΕΧΝΟΣ: Some Fundamental Ideas of Aristarchus on Homer as a Poet,' *Mnemosyne* 23:2. 1970. pp 162 & 176. Cf. also Scholia *A* 19.365-368a where Aristarchus is reported to have decided to delete his earlier *obelos* sign athetising a phrase, having decided upon its inclusion ποιητικὸν νομίσαντα τὸ τοιοῦτο. Aristarchus' view of Homer in this respect is noted by Rudolf Pfeiffer in his famous, *History of Classical Scholarship: From the Beginnings to the End of the Hellenistic Age* (Clarendon Press: Oxford. 1968), pp 230-231. 'If the Iliad and Odyssey were to be esteemed as creations of perfect workmanship by one poet, not a few difficulties and discrepancies presented themselves to the scrutinising scholarly mind. It was relatively easy to recognise and to remove lines missing in some of the manuscripts as post-Homeric insertions. But there were many lines or even passages in all the manuscripts which seemed hardly reconcilable with the idea of perfection and unity...The only solution was not to delete them, but to mark them as spurious, as 'interpolations' (τὸ ἀθετεῖν); athetesis, invented by his predecessors, was practised by Aristarchus with the utmost skill.' It is likely that Aristarchus and his predecessors developed this use of 'authorial intention' from some of Aristotle's literary theory. See, for example, *Poet.* 1448b23-27: Διεσπάσθη δὲ κατὰ τὰ οἰκεῖα ἤθη ἡ ποίησις οἱ μὲν γὰρ σεμνότεροι τὰς καλὰς ἐμιμοῦντο πράξεις καὶ τὰς τῶν τοιούτων, οἱ δὲ εὐτελέστεροι τὰς τῶν φαύλων, πρῶτον ψόγους ποιοῦντες, ὥσπερ ἕτεροι ὕμνους καὶ ἐγκώμια. Aristotle continues to illustrate this claim by referring to Homer's preeminent ability as a poet. Likewise, in *Poet.* 1460a6, Aristotle gives unique credit to

A similar argument is employed in Hebrews 4:6-8. Here, it is not so much the identity of the author of the Old Testament passage cited which is important, but the time when he wrote it. The issue at stake in this passage, as in the larger treatment of Psalm 95:7-11 in Hebrews 3-4, is whether the promise of entering into God's rest still stands for first Century believers in Christ. The author of Hebrews uses a number of arguments to show that the threat in Psalm 95:11 of non-entry into God's rest is one which should urge Christians on to persevere in their faith. Firstly, God's rest still stands open because the wilderness generation to whom the threat was first made (not through Psalm 95, but in the historical occasion to which the Psalm refers) failed to enter that rest (Hebrews 3:16-19).[58] Secondly, God's rest is open to believers because it represents not a promised land but a time of Sabbath seen in God's own rest after the creation of the world (Hebrews 4:3-5).[59] Finally, God's rest stands open to believers because it is held out in the form of a threat of non-entry at the time of David, a time when many would assume that God's people might

---

Homer for realising the true, hidden place of the poet's voice: "Ὅμηρος δὲ ἄλλα τε πολλὰ ἄξιος ἐπαινεῖσθαι καὶ δὴ καὶ ὅτι μόνος τῶν ποιητῶν οὐκ ἀγνοεῖ ὃ δεῖ ποιεῖν αὐτόν. (This is an interesting observation since 'Alexandrian poetry is highly self-conscious, the poet's voice is often heard through the poem.' George A. Kennedy and Doreen C. Innes, 'Hellenistic Literary and Philosophical Scholarship,' in *The Cambridge History of Literary Criticism, Vol I: Classical Criticism*, Ed. George A. Kennedy (CUP: Cambridge. 1989), p 202.

[58] It is interesting that the author of Hebrews makes two different uses of history in his treatment of Palm 95. This first use understands the psalm to *refer* to an event in history (which Randall C. Gleason, 'The Old Testament Background of Rest in Hebrews 3:7-4:11,' *Bibliotheca Sacra* 157. 2000. p 290 persuasively argues pertains primarily to Numbers 14). Even though the author understands the psalm to be written much later than this event, the historic referent of the text still influences its interpretation. The author draws a distinction between content and setting. The author essentially argues that the historical content of the psalm is correct, supporting its ability to hold out rest as a promise which remains open: God's people really did fail to enter the land, proving that unbelief may yet be the cause of 1st Century failure to enter God's rest.

[59] Marie E. Isaacs, *Sacred Space: An Approach to the Theology of the Epistle to the Hebrews* (SAP: Sheffield. 1992), p 88 and Matthew Thiessen, 'Hebrews and the End of the Exodus,' *Novum Testamentum* 49:4. 2007. p 358.

already be enjoying God's rest by inhabiting the promised land of Palestine.

> Therefore, since it remained possible for some to enter into [God's rest], and those who had first had the good news proclaimed to them did not enter due to faithlessness, again [God] appointed a certain day, 'today', by David, saying after a great deal of time, as it is said, 'today if you hear his voice, do not harden your hearts.' For if Joshua had given them rest, he would not have spoken about another day after this (Hebrews 4:6-8).

The author of Hebrews connects the Psalm to David, following traditional attestation,[60] and uses an understanding of when David lived to work out what 'my rest' means in the Psalm. The author of Hebrews knew that Psalm 95, with its promise of rest, originated, then, later than the wilderness generation and later even than Joshua, who led the people of Israel into the promised land. If the Psalm came after this entry, entry into the promised land cannot constitute entry into God's rest. God was still to promise his rest in the time of David with the promised land firmly occupied. This argument would not work if the Psalm could not be claimed to be later than Joshua and the entry of God's people into the promised land. But because the promise is renewed at a time when it might be thought to be meaningless, the understanding of God's rest as the land of Palestine is shown to be false. David's time of speaking Psalm 95 is crucial.[61]

---

[60] Erich Grässer, *An die Hebräer: Hebr 1-6* (Benziger/Neukirchener: Zürich. 1990), p 213.
[61] Paul Ellingworth, *The Epistle to the Hebrews: A Commentary on the Greek Text* (Eerdmans: Grand Rapids. 1993), p 253. R. T. France, 'The Writer of the Hebrews as a Biblical Expositor,' *Tyndale Bulletin* 47:2. 1996. p 271 'Because the psalmist, writing centuries after the exodus events, could still appeal for response 'today,' the writer infers that the rest he refers to cannot be only a lost opportunity in the distant past, but remains available to the people of God.' See also, Graham Hughes, *Hebrews and Hermeneutics: The Epistle to the Hebrews as a New Testament Example of Biblical Interpretation* (CUP: Cambridge. 1979), p 43. 'In fact the promise...or gospel...are regarded as being identical for both communities. One can only speak of a 'Neue Heilssituation' in the very limited sense that the renewal of the promise (i.e., the same one) in the time of David testifies that it is still intact.'

The argument enables the author of Hebrews to come to the encouraging conclusion in 4:9: 'Therefore, there remains a Sabbath rest for the people of God'.

This appeal to the historical setting of the author lacks clear precedent in the literature most often thought to have influenced how New Testament authors interpreted Old Testament passages. Susan E. Docherty, in her significant and recent monograph arguing for a rabbinic influence on the use of the Old Testament in Hebrews writes,

> The author's exegesis depends also on his employment of an argument from chronology in Hebrews 4:8-9, where he explains his view that 'rest' must mean 'Sabbath rest', not 'entry into the land of Canaan', on the basis that the psalm promising rest as something in the future was spoken long after the wilderness period, when the Israelites were settled in the land (Hebrews 4:8). This interpretative technique...points to a difference between the New Testament and several other examples of early Jewish biblical exegesis, which on the whole display little interest in the historical background of scriptural passages. The rabbinic maxim: 'There is no before or after in scripture' is well known.[62]

---

[62] Susan E. Docherty, *The Use of the Old Testament in Hebrews: A Case Study in Early Jewish Bible Interpretation* (Mohr Siebeck: Tübingen. 2009), p 192. A similar argument employing 'chronology' is used in Hebrews 7:11 to explain Psalm 110:4. Here, the installation of a priest according to the order of Melchizedek is seen to come later than the scriptural command instituting the Levitical priesthood. The later modifies or annuls the earlier. As with Psalm 95, the dating of the text being discussed is of some interpretative importance. See James Moffatt, *A Critical and Exegetical Commentary on the Epistle to the Hebrews* (T. & T. Clark: Edinburgh. 1975) p 96 'The inference that the νόμος is antiquated for Christians reaches the same end as Paul does by his dialectic, but by a very different route. Ἀνίστασθαι...and λέγεσθαι refer to Psalm 110:4, which is regarded as marking a new departure.' See also F.F. Bruce, *The Epistle to the Hebrews*, (Marshall, Morgan and Scott: London and Edinburgh. 1964.) p 143 'It could not be argued that the latter priesthood (of Aaron) superseded the earlier (of Melchizedek); for when the priesthood of Aaron was well established the divine oracle was uttered which hailed the Messiah of David's line as "a priest after the order of Melchizedek."'

The use of ideas about authorship when interpreting Scripture is a distinctive feature of the New Testament's treatment of the Old Testament. Because of this, it is very difficult to dismiss it as something which belongs to an anti-Christian way of thinking. It is a clear part of the Christian inheritance, a feature of the use of Scripture in the earliest Church. But it could also be more than that. It is commonplace in scholarship on the New Testament's use of the Old Testament to attempt to identify sources or traditions behind particular examples of Scriptural interpretation in the New Testament. In the case of the two passages discussed above which use arguments which look for something akin to authorial intent, there has been little success in identifying plausible sources or background traditions. Yet neither of these passages are the earliest Christian example of explaining Scripture in relation to authorship. It could be that this way of interpreting Scripture is rooted in the biblical interpretation of the Lord Jesus himself. In Mark 12:35-37 (a pericope found in Luke and Matthew too, often conveniently referred to as the *Davidssohnfrage*), Jesus explores the identity of the Messiah as the Son of David. Whilst the passage is complicated and scholars do not agree on what precisely Jesus is claiming about the Messiah, Jesus' way of interpreting Scripture is interesting.[63] Jesus interprets   Psalm

---

[63] Scholarly disagreement largely relates to whether or not Jesus is denying that the Messiah is the Son of David, though the very meaning of the title 'Son of David' is disputed too. If Jesus is denying that the Messiah is the Son of David, as may be the most straightforward reading of the passage, why is it that Matthew details Jesus' descent from David in his genealogy? Such a denial seems to contradict what is usually thought of as a central feature of New Testament Christology, seen particularly in Romans 1:3 and 2 Timothy 2:8. It is more likely that Jesus simply questions something about the nature of the Messiah's Davidic sonship: principally that the Messianic Son of David is in fact David's Lord. For a variety of views see Evald Lövestam, 'Jésus fils de David chez les Synoptiques,' *Studia Theologica* 28:1. 1974, Kim Paffenroth, 'Jesus as Anointed and Healing Son of David in the Gospel of Matthew,' *Biblica* 80:4. 1999, Francis J. Moloney, 'The Re-interpretation of Psalm VIII and the Son of Man Debate,' *New Testament Studies* 27:5. 1981, Fritz Neugebauer, 'Die Davidssohnfrage (Mark XII. 35-7 Parr.) und der Menschensohn,' *New Testament Studies* 21:1. 1974 and Yigal Levin, '"Son of God" and "Son of David": The "Adoption" of Jesus into the Davidic Line,' *Journal for the Study of the New Testament* 28:4. 2006.

110:1 by putting the text on the lips of its author, David. Jesus asks how the Messiah can be David's son if David himself calls him his Lord in Psalm 110:1. In asking this question, Jesus shows that according to Scripture, the Messiah is someone greater than David, even if he is known as the 'Son of David.' This way of interpreting Scripture is much like that of Hebrews 4:7 and Acts 2:29-31: the text's meaning is understood in relation to who the author is. Such interpretation asks, 'who is the author of the text and what could he mean by the words he uses, given what is known about him?' Interest in authorial intention is certainly not a recent feature of biblical interpretation.

Of course, it can be maintained that there are genres of writing in which authorial intention is not important, usually because the author has deliberately *intended* for readers to come up with their own interpretations of his or her work. Yet, it would seem that every type of biblical literature reflects a clear concern to communicate a particular thing. Luke's and John's Gospels, for example, both state very clearly why they have been written and what it is hoped they will achieve as pieces of communication.[64] There is no reason to think that Matthew and Mark lack similar intent, though not stated explicitly. Similarly, the Epistles and the prophetic literature, and to some extent the apocalyptic literature, set out to address specific issues, such as apostasy or immorality.

But can the author really be known? It's all very well insisting that an author's intention ought to drive interpretation, but what if knowledge of an author is lost across an unbridgeable gulf of history? What if the author cannot be known? The idea that authors cannot be meaningfully known, especially if they are long dead and lived in a culture very different to our own, is a common objection to an exegetical focus upon authorial intention. Those who maintain this criticism often refer to the 'intentionalist fallacy': the seemingly naïve notion that an author and his or her intention can be known just as one might know one's own intention. So to what extent can an author

---

[64] John 20:30-31 and Luke 1:1-4.

be known after two thousand years? Does authorial intention actually rely upon a great deal of imagination?[65] George A. Lindbeck argues that

> the distinction to be maintained [in authorial intention] is between why and what, between the speaker's act of intending a speech act (why she spoke) and the speech act's intentionality (what she intended to say). Appeal to authorial intention in the first sense is illicit, an intentional fallacy, while in the second, it is not only legitimate but necessary; without this appeal there is no exit from the text, that is, no non arbitrary way of discerning which of its many possible senses is the true or most plausible one.[66]

For Lindbeck, the quest for authorial intention ought to focus upon what can be known from the text itself. In the case of the Bible, texts are smothered in information about their authors and why they wrote, whether the author is named or not. One only has to look at the kind of language, literary devices, common themes, structure and imagery used to get a sense of why a text has been written. In some cases, such as Luke 1:1-4, a biblical author can be quite explicit about why they have written. This makes the belief far from fallacious that an author's intention can be known. In fact, Luke is a particularly good example of a biblical author who is known almost exclusively through the texts he has written. Any scholarly attempt to discern Luke's aims in writing completely depend on his 'speech act': Luke-Acts. Luke is unknowable as an author if his texts are not considered.

---

[65] The use of imagination is by no means a bad thing. As Trevor Hart, 'Imagination and Responsible Reading,' in *Renewing Biblical Interpretation*, Ed., Craig G. Bartholomew, Colin Greene and Karl Möller (Grand Rapids/Carlisle: Zondervan/Paternoster. 2000), pp 307-308 argues, through imagination we stand a greater chance of seeing the Bible as something other than our own ideas and prejudices as we attempt to consider the distant author's aim in writing.

[66] George A. Lindbeck, 'Postcritical Canonical Interpretation: Three Modes of Retrieval,' in *Theological Exegesis: Essays in Honor of Brevard S. Childs*, Ed. Kathryn Green-McCreight and Christopher Seitz (Grand Rapids: Eerdmans. 1999), p 49.

So then, the aim to grasp authorial intention begins and remains with the text for which it is sought and in which it is evidenced.

4.2. How we can benefit from seeking authorial intention

So far in this chapter, I have simply tried to show that a hermeneutic of authorial intent is both theologically plausible and practically possible. However, it must be said that the attempt to read the Bible as something that bears a special relation to a specific set of historical circumstances out of which and for which it was written, is also enormously beneficial to Christians. The great danger of many of the recent attempts to approach the Bible 'theologically' is the great temptation to discover in Scripture only those ideas with which we are already comfortable. This is the danger that is often termed 'eisegesis'. According to Barton, eisegesis is a regrettable and prominent feature of so-called Theological Interpretation of Scripture.[67]

Some of these 'theological' readers of the Bible give priority to a rule of faith, a doctrinal lens through which biblical texts are interpreted.[68] Rules of faith are often authoritative theological texts, such as the Nicene Creed or the Westminster Confession, but may simply be a particular understanding of the Gospel. This is certainly

---

[67] Barton, *Biblical Criticism*, pp 164-167

[68] Such as George A. Lindbeck, 'The Story-Shaped Church: Critical Exegesis and Theological Interpretation,' in Stephen E. Fowl (ed.), *The Theological Interpretation of Scripture: Classic and Contemporary Readings* (Blackwell: Oxford. 1997), p 41. The idea of the controlling rule of faith can be seen behind many theological approaches to reading Scripture. Canonical interpretation, which is discussed below, at a popular level, often features a claim to interpret Scripture according to a certain understanding of what the Bible's message is. This understanding of its message, perhaps abstracted from a certain reading of a few key texts, becomes, in a sense, a rule by which particular 'difficult' passages are interpreted. A good example of this occurred in the final episode of the excellent 2009 BBC series *A History of Christianity*, presented by Diarmaid MacCulloch, in which the Revd Nicholas Holtam (Vicar of St Martin in the Fields) describes the essence of the Bible's message as 'God is love': a message which he considers urges the full acceptance of practicing homosexuals at every level of Church governance.

the sense in which the rule of faith was articulated by Tertullian in the 2nd Century, possibly the earliest extant reference to the concept. The truth of the Gospel was seen by Tertullian as a guide to the interpretation of Scripture. Readings of Scripture which could not be reconciled to the Gospel of Christ were to be rejected.[69] Yet a rule of faith is not necessarily a guarantee of interpretation as there are potential pitfalls in its use: whilst a rule of faith may be a biblically orthodox set of beliefs, there is nothing to stop it being a heretical set of beliefs, chosen at the whim of the interpreter. When a rule of faith is established, it is very hard for it to be challenged by Scripture itself. Whilst most proponents of the use of a rule of faith agree that it must be open to revision in the light of Scripture, in practice this openness is hard to achieve. Whilst there is no truly neutral way of approaching Scripture, giving priority to the rule of faith places undue power in the hands of the interpreter, firstly to decide the lens through which Scripture must be read, then to impose that lens, that standard on Scripture itself. Against such a rule, the Bible's freedom to speak that which is not already believed by the interpreter is limited.

A similar hermeneutic to those which employ a rule of faith, is offered by the various approaches to biblical interpretation which are influenced by the pragmatism of Stanley Fish and others. Rather than a set of doctrines operating as an interpretive rule, scholars influenced by philosophical pragmatism place the perceived needs of a particular community at the heart of interpretation. Usually this community is that in which the reading takes place, typically a local church in a specific local context. This approach ought to be commended for taking seriously the need to relate the reading of the Bible to real life as experienced by real people. However, the danger of eisegesis is rarely taken seriously by proponents of this approach. Through this approach, the Bible is virtually powerless to challenge its readers except in ways already determined by the community.

Stephen Fowl, for example, argues that biblical interpretation ought to affirm the local community, producing readings which will

---

[69] Tertullian, *The Prescription against Heretics*, XIX.

have a positive impact on that community.[70] One can hardly argue against that. Yet how does one decide what is for the benefit of the community? In Fowl's case, only truly 'inclusive' readings of the Bible can be beneficial. Biblical passages which seem to undermine this inclusivity must be read in the light of the overwhelming need for inclusivity to be proclaimed. The perceived need of the community becomes something of a rule of faith. The question is, though, who decides what is beneficial to the community? Fowl's vision is probably very different to my own. If a community's sense of what is good and bad determines what can be read from the Bible, is there any point in reading the Bible at all? Will the Bible at any point be allowed to challenge existing prejudices?

Theological Interpretation of Scripture which follows pragmatic lines can severely limit the reading of the Bible to what is already agreed upon as acceptable by the community in which it is read. But, as Evangelicals, we are often guilty of propagating a similarly limited approach to reading the Bible, particularly in relation to how we apply the Bible to ourselves. For example, we often limit application of passages to certain applications that have a sort of communally accepted status. How often at the end of a not particularly engaged Bible study is the question asked, 'and how does this passage make a difference to your life'? Often the answer runs, 'I need to pray/trust God/read the Bible/share the Gospel with my non-Christian friends more.' These are often good and proper applications, but they are easy applications, ones made easy by the communal sense in our churches that these things are important. It's right to see the Bible urging us to do more of these things, but their acceptance in the church community can make them flow from a passage without any serious thought about the passage and without any serious searching of one's heart to see where the challenge hits home specifically. Having a set of popular applications, even if they are good applications, impoverishes Bible study by limiting the challenge readers are likely to face when they read Scripture.

---

[70] Fowl, *Engaging Scripture*, p 403

47

The other feature of some Theological Interpretation of Scripture which can be seen to limit the challenge posed by biblical study is the use of the biblical Canon as an interpretative aid. Canonical interpretation which views particular passages in relation to the rest of the canon of Holy Scripture is one of the most long-standing approaches within the Theological Interpretation of Scripture tendency. Major exponents of canonical interpretation include Brevard Childs, Walter Moberly, Christopher Seitz and Robert Jenson. The idea of explaining biblical texts using other biblical texts is very good and appropriate to the common divine authorship of the Scriptures and the common story of God's grace they tell. To some extent, New Testament authors follow this practice of interpreting Old Testament texts by referring to others. For example, in the discussion of Psalm 95 in Hebrews 3-4 which was examined earlier in this chapter, the author of Hebrews introduces Genesis 2:2 to further define the nature of God's rest in Psalm 95.

> For [God] has said somewhere of the seventh day: 'and God rested on the seventh day from all his work [Genesis 2:2]'. And in this place again, 'they shall not enter into my rest [Psalm 95:11]'.

The author of Hebrews attempts to clarify the meaning of 'my rest' in Psalm 95 by comparing the concept with another instance in Scripture where God's own rest or resting is implied. This shows some degree of precision, since there are many examples of the use of the word 'rest' in Old Testament, but what marks its use in Psalm 95:11 is that it is '*my* rest'. The author uses this comparison to demonstrate that the rest which remains open to the people of God is not that provided by some promised land, but rather is something heavenly: a Sabbath rest enjoyed by God himself. This method of comparison is known as *gezerah shewah* and is a well-attested feature of the earliest extant rabbinic interpretation of Scripture. Behind such rabbinic techniques is an understanding of Scripture as a consistent whole, a universe made of text governed by its own rules and only really possible to understand on its own terms.

Canonical Interpretation is very good and has much to commend itself. Evangelicals in particular ought to feel a significant

48

sense of sympathy with this approach to interpreting the Bible.[71] After all, the Bible is a unified document, no matter how diverse it may seem. And its unity is not simply due to the process of canonisation. Much of the Bible is interwoven, as New Testament authors reflect on Old Testament texts and use Old Testament typology and as Old Testament authors wrote with the expectation that theirs was not the final word.[72]

But the difficulty comes when the unity of Scripture drowns out its diversity. When we read a particular biblical passage through a canonical lens, the lens of our perception of the whole of Scripture, it is possible to miss the particular contribution that text may be making. In other words, we may interpret a biblical passage in such a

---

[71] Indeed it is a prominent feature of Reformed Theology. See, for example, the Westminster Confession 1:9; 'The infallible rule of interpretation of Scripture is the Scripture itself: and therefore, when there is a question about the true and full sense of any Scripture (which is not manifold, but one), it must be searched and known by other places that speak more clearly.' Note here, also, the rejection of the notion of indeterminacy. See also articles VII and XX of the XXXIX Articles of Religion.

[72] It is clear that authors and redactors of such texts as 2 Kings, 2 Chronicles and Nehemiah (as well as other texts which do not end great narrative sequences) did not see themselves as producing 'stand-alone' work. Each of these texts is dependent upon certain texts which precede it, but more importantly none of them end with any sense of finality: they each end expecting something more from the narrative of God's dealings with his people. James A. Montgomery, *A Critical and Exegetical Commentary on the Books of Kings* (T. & T. Clark: Edinburgh. 1951), p.567 'The book is thus concluded with the theme of the continued dignity of the house of David, with what hope in mind we may only surmise.' Cf. Richard Bauckham, 'Reading Scripture as a Coherent Story,' in *The Art of Reading Scripture*, Ed., Ellen F. Davis and Richard B. Hays (Eerdmans: Grand Rapids. 2003), pp 38-45 for an alternative approach to this problem which attempts to take the historically contingent nature of the biblical literature seriously.

way as its author would not recognise.[73] The particular challenge to God's people made in the past by the Holy Spirit through that author would be lost to us. The question remains: once we have worked out what the Canon has to say, will the Bible ever say anything to us again? Won't it just repeat what we already know: the canonical lens through which we read it?

The great problem with the rule of faith, pragmatic hermeneutics and canonical interpretation is that they can overwhelm particular texts of the Bible with a whole set of preconceived notions of what those texts are 'permitted' to mean. Our ability to be genuinely challenged by the Bible's teaching can be stifled by such interpretative rules which attempt to limit interpretation by what we already hold to be true and important. This objection to such reading practices is not due to a desire to encourage diversity in interpretation. As was argued above, a single authoritative meaning ought to be sought for each passage in line with its communicative function as an historically contingent piece of revelation. What needs to be preserved by biblical hermeneutics is our ability to be surprised and challenged by what the Bible says, which will not happen if interpretation is always made safe by a rule of faith or something similar. When we read the Bible in that way, we will always encounter our own beliefs and values in its pages.

Authorial intent and the exegetical techniques which aim to disclose it represent the possibility of interpretation which allows the

---

[73] This is the criticism made by John Barton, *Reading the Old Testament: Method in Biblical Study* (DLT: London. 1984), pp 77-103. Cf. Cf. Robert P. Gordon, 'A Warranted Version of Historical Criticism? A Response to Alvin Plantinga,' in *"Behind" the Text: History and Biblical Interpretation*, Ed., Craig Bartholomew, C. Stephen Evans, Mary Healy and Murray Rae (Paternoster/Zondervan: Carlisle/Michigan. 2003), p 83. Robert Jenson provides one of the clearest examples of reading one's theology into texts which could not possibly have been intended to express such ideas when originally written. Jenson's *Ezekiel* (SCM: London. 2009) contain Jenson's most distinct ideas, such as his Christological development of the *Shekinah*, already laid out in his *Systematic Theology, Volume 1: The Triune God* (OUP: Oxford. 1997), p 78. Cf. idem., *The Triune Identity: God According to the Gospel* (Wipf & Stock: Eugene. 2002), pp 33-40.

Bible to say things which we may not yet believe, to express ideas which are far from our own. This is not to say, as the historical-critical scholars did, that when one looks for the historical meaning of a text one can do so as a neutral enquirer, completely open to whatever the author may be saying through his creation. We can never be as neutral as we may fancy ourselves. Sin prevents it. If I think the Bible's teaching on a particular aspect of my sin is unclear, perhaps because there is no consensus on it, I am likely always to read the Bible in such a way as to leave that aspect of my sin unscathed. We cannot approach the Bible neutrally. ↘ *what about prior teaching etc.?*

But we can approach the Bible in humility, with hearts and minds graciously opened by the Holy Spirit, who, despite all this discussion of hermeneutics, is our sole means of access to the voice of God in his word. As sinners made humble by the Spirit we can approach the Bible with the hope that in it we read voices not our own. These voices, because they belong to others, to particular human authors whom we seek to recognise and affirm in their difference to us, can never be made to conform to our wills as readers. Paul Joyce, in celebration of historical criticism, writes,

> There is even a spiritual dimension for me in being confronted by the 'other' of the text as laid bare by historical criticism. The text is not me, it is not my projection or an extension of my own psychology; rather it challenges me from beyond myself in a way that commands humility... There is moreover an ethical dimension to historical-critical reading: firm rooting of a text in its original context may help guard against 'exploitative' reading.[74]

The passages discussed above which feature a desire to articulate some form of authorial intention also feature as strong desire to challenge readers and the interpretations they already have.

---

[74] Paul Joyce, 'Proverbs 8 in Interpretation (1): Historical Criticism and Beyond,' in *Reading Texts, Seeking Wisdom*, Ed. David E. Ford and Graham Stanton (SCM: London. 2003), p 95.

Hebrews 4 clearly argues against a particular view of God's rest as temporal. The author of Hebrews shows that an understanding of the 'rest' in Psalm 95 as the land of Palestine is historically implausible. It is historically implausible because it was written by David (through the Holy Spirit) in David's own time, when the threat of non-entry into Palestine would be meaningless. The author of Hebrews' argument from the authorship of the psalm challenges his readers false view of God's rest, a view which may have tempted them to turn away from the living God because of an unbelieving heart (Hebrews 3:12). Of course, many readings of Psalm 95 could be challenged in some other way – it is not the aim of the author's interpretation of the psalm simply to say something different or controversial. The value of the challenge his faithful interpretation of the psalm offers is that it is demonstrably not made up to suit his own needs. It is historically persuasive. A good reason is offered for it. Likewise, the interpretation of Psalm 16 in Acts 2 undermines existing assumptions about what that psalm meant. Whilst it is difficult to know whether this reflects a standard reading in the 1st Century, *Psalms Midrash* 16 records an interpretation of the psalm as being about David. This interpretation probably was popular in the 1st Century as it appears to be argued against by Peter in his Pentecost sermon.[75] Peter's reference to the psalm's Davidic authorship deliberately undermines this interpretation, presenting something far more challenging, whilst, at the same time, more historically plausible to his audience. The relocation of Scripture to its historical context enables it to be something other than what we might want it to be.

---

[75] Cf. Donald Juel, 'Social Dimensions of Exegesis: The Use of Psalm 16 in Acts 2,' *CBQ* 43. 1981. pp 547-548 and 555.

5.   Weren't things so different in those days?

J. P. Gabler, the 18th Century Biblical Scholar, thought that by interpreting the Bible as an historical document, looking for authorial intention, Christian doctrine would become less controversial.

> Thus, as soon as all these things have been properly observed and carefully arranged, at last a clear sacred Scripture will be selected with scarcely any doubtful readings, made up of passages which are appropriate to the Christian religion of all times. These passages will show with unambiguous words the form of faith that is truly divine; the *dicta classica* properly so called, which can then be laid out as the fundamental basis for a more subtle dogmatic scrutiny. For only from these methods can those certain and undoubted universal ideas be singled out, those ideas which alone are useful in dogmatic theology.[76]

There is something quite concrete about biblical interpretation which takes the historical setting of biblical texts seriously. Even if we can't agree what an author intended in a particular case, there are least ways of ruling out certain historically implausible readings. Of course, in such cases, our failure to agree will be entirely our own fault: there is little internal ambiguity in the biblical texts themselves.[77] But supposing, as Gabler suggests, that Christians agree on what an author intended with a certain passage, does that make interpretation simple? As mentioned above, biblical interpretation often features a 'special hermeneutic', something which makes biblical interpretation different from the interpretation of other texts.

---

[76] John Sandys-Wunsch and Laurence Eldridge, 'J. P. Gabler and the Distinction between Biblical and Dogmatic Theology: Translation, Commentary and Discussion of his Originality,' *SJT* 33:2. 1980. p 143.

[77] On the subject of the perspicuity or clarity of Scripture, see my 'John 4:1-42 and the Clarity of the Bible,' *Churchman* 123:3. 2009.

Because the Bible is Scripture (a text through which the voice of God is to be heard in some way) to most of its readers, interpretation does not end with consensus about what St Paul or St John meant in a particular passage.

Biblical interpretation always involves working out the meaning of a passage for those who are to be challenged by it today. Biblical interpretation, when undertaken by Christians, can never be a purely historical exercise: it always matters deeply what St Paul or St John meant. So what happens when Christians agree that St Paul meant a certain thing when he wrote a certain passage but what St Paul meant seems horribly unpalatable to most in contemporary society? To what extent can the intentions of biblical authors be dismissed, or treated with a pinch of salt, on account of when they expressed them? This question has been put to me a number of times. One example which comes to mind went as follows: 'you know all that stuff Paul wrote about women in leadership? Isn't that mainly down to the culture he was living in back then? Surely that doesn't apply to us now, does it?' Here, there's no disagreement that Paul has something to say about women's leadership which jars with the dominant contemporary view. No, what's at stake is how that very clear historically plausible meaning should be applied to the day-to-day activity of leading the body of Christ, the Church.

5.1.   Limitations of historical contextualisation

An understanding of Scripture as historically contingent, as something which should be interpreted in the light of the historical context in and for which it was first written, can have both a positive and a negative effect upon how it is interpreted. I hope the positives were put across persuasively in the previous chapter. The principal negative effect historical interpretation can entail is the severance of the past from the present. Often, the more we know about the past, the less it seems to relate to the present. Often it seems that there is such a great cultural, political, social and religious difference between the past and the present that the writers of the past have little to offer to us in the present. Historical study of ancient texts can open up a vast and unbridgeable gap between the past and the present. This is

54

particularly the case in the natural sciences. Few contemporary scientists would say that Aristotle or Hippocrates gave the last word in their subject, except perhaps in a philosophical or ethical sense. Clearly our understanding of the mechanics of how the natural world functions has advanced to such a degree that the writings of such ancient thinkers seem ludicrous. Can the same be said of the Bible when viewed from a 21st Century perspective? To what extent does the passage of time erect a barrier between the text and its contemporary readers? If there is a barrier, can it be scaled or broken down?

This problem in hermeneutics is referred to using the technical term *distanciation*. Distanciation refers to the way in which a text is related to its reader, whether it is read as addressing the reader personally or as addressing a situation of less or no relevance to that reader. Christians have often read the Bible with little sense of distanciation – in other words, they have read it as though there were no distance between themselves and the text perceived as addressing them personally. Often this comes at the cost of understanding the historical and literal sense of the Bible as the personal context of the reader becomes predominant. Historical Criticism went the other way, creating a vast gulf between the Bible and its modern reader, a gulf made out of history.[78] Whilst the early historical critical scholars were no doubt right to think themselves out of their own contexts into the world in which biblical texts were written, historical criticism went on to provide readings of biblical literature which contributed nothing to the task of living as a disciple of Jesus two thousand years

---

[78] This is something noted by Paul Ricoeur, 'The Hermeneutical Function of Distanciation,' in *From Text to Action: Essays in Hermeneutics, II*, trans. Kathleen Blamey and John B. Thompson (London: Continuum. 2008), p 72. Ricoeur, here, talks about an opposition between 'alienating distanciation and belonging. This opposition is an antinomy because it establishes an untenable alternative: on the one hand, alienating distanciation is the attitude that renders possible the objectification that reigns in the human sciences; but on the other hand, this distanciation, which is the condition of the scientific status of the sciences, is at the same time the fall that destroys the fundamental and primordial relation whereby we belong to and participate in the historical reality that we claim to construct as an object.'

after his ascension. Later on, when the beliefs and practices of ordinary Christians were mentioned, they were brought up to be maligned or as sacred cows to be destroyed. At the same time, some historical-critical scholars believed in orthodox Christianity despite a firm conviction that such beliefs were inconsistent with their understanding of the historical Jesus or true Pauline Christology etc. Conservative Evangelicalism in its post World War Two form has tried to articulate a form of distanciation which is half-way between the two extremes of individualistic reading and irrelevant historicism. A standard exegetical approach would be to ask two different but overlapping questions of the biblical text: 'what did this mean for them then?' and 'so what does this mean for us now?'[79] This assumes that the historically intended meaning of a text is foundational for its interpretation in the present. It assumes that the application of the text in the present grows out of its meaning in the past. This is a much more nuanced approach to distanciation. But if the past is different from the present as the two questions suggest, what reason is there for using the past as the basis for application in the present?

5.2. Clues from Scripture

Here the New Testament offers some helpful clues to how an ancient text can be taken to speak in the present. Again, this is seen in the use of the Old Testament in the New Testament. A biblical hermeneutic using appropriate distanciation affirms two important aspects to the biblical text: its relation to a person or period in history and the divine inspiration which enables it to be God's word in situations other than that in which it was originally written or uttered. This dual nature of the biblical text can be seen in many of the phrases used to introduce

---

[79]   Adam, *Speaking God's Words*, pp 97-102

Old Testament quotations in the New Testament.[80] Often, this dual nature is indicated in such phrases as 'this was to fulfill what was spoken through (διὰ) the prophet Isaiah', to cite a typical Matthean example. Scripture is spoken by God through someone else, someone whose identity is considered to be important enough to mention. In other places, these introductory phrases, or citation formulae as they are usually termed in New Testament Studies, are more explicit. Consider Acts 28:25, 'the Holy Spirit spoke well to your fathers through Isaiah the prophet' or Mark 12:35 (paralleled in the other Synoptic Gospels) 'David himself said through the Holy Spirit'. In the case of Acts 28:25, Paul (from whose speech in Rome this phrase comes) identifies a passage from Isaiah 6 as being given to a certain group of people in the past, by the Holy Spirit, through a particular prophetic author. Yet the quotation is still used by Paul as something which communicates truth from God to people who could never meet Isaiah due to their own situation in history. The fact that Scripture has an historical origin, that it was given in and through real situations and people of the past, provides no barrier to its authority

---

[80] Examples include Matthew 3:3, 4:14, 8:17, 12:17, 13:35, 21:4, 22:43, Mark 12:36, Luke 20:42, Acts 2:16, 4:25, 28:31, Romans 9:25 and Hebrews 4:7. See Adam, *Speaking God's Words*, p 105 on Hebrews 3-4 particularly. Of course, there are many more examples in the New Testament which cite just one of these aspects of the text, such as the prophet or book it came from or its status as the direct speech of God. Prominent examples of the former can be found in Romans 9-11 where David, Isaiah, Moses and Hosea are mentioned as authors of quotations. Hebrews provides many examples of the latter, particularly in the scriptural catena of 1:5-13 which posits all its biblical quotations as God's own speech. It is striking, therefore, that it is in this letter that some of the New Testament's clearest witness to the idea of Scripture as historically contingent (as something to be explained with reference to the historical context from which it came) is available.

in the present. Scripture is seen in these citation formulae as having both divine and human aspects.[81]

This is also the understanding of Scripture's inspiration seen in 2 Peter 1:19-21, an important text for understanding inspiration generally. Peter asserts that the 'word of the prophets' has been confirmed by the eyewitness testimony of the apostles.

> And we have the word of the prophets confirmed, which [word] it is good for you to hold on to, as it is as a light shining in a murky place until the day dawns and the morning star rises in your hearts. Know this first: that every prophecy of Scripture came not from [a prophet's] own imaginings. For prophecy never came by the will of a man, but, being carried along by the Holy Spirit, men spoke from God (2 Peter 1:19-21).

Peter argues here against a view of the prophets' word which sees it simply as the word of human beings. Richard Bauckham, whose commentary on Jude and 2 Peter is widely regarded as one of the best commentaries on these books in existence, writes,

> The author's appeal to the authority of OT prophecy in

---

[81] It is easy for this popular description of the nature of biblical literature to sound blasphemous because of the Christological comparison it elicits. Needless to say, the concept of Scripture's dual authorship is quite different to orthodox biblical Christology. To defend the dual nature of Scripture from the charge that it elevates the Bible to the position which should be exclusively that of the Lord Jesus, one needs to stress the importance of the idea of agency. Any relation to divinity Scripture enjoys exists purely because Scripture, like its human authors, is understood as something God uses. So for example, God's written word has some degree of power and sovereignty. This is not its own, but exists because God uses his word to achieve his own sovereign ends. Hebrews 4:12-13 provides a clear statement of the sovereign role of Scripture in God's sovereign purpose. It is God's word which exposes the human heart and cuts into the places hidden to others, yet v.13 concludes that the disclosing activity of the word exists because 'nothing is hidden before [God]' before whom all creation will be called to account. Similarly, God's word is righteous because God himself is so (Psalm 119:137).

support of the expectation of the Parousia (v 19) must now be defended against a second objection made by the opponents. They rejected the authority of OT prophecy by denying its divine origin. They said that while it may be true that the prophets received signs and dreams and vision, their prophecies were their own human interpretations of these, not God-given interpretations.[82]

The problem with the way Peter's opponents understood prophecy was not that they disagreed with Peter over what the prophets were saying. The problem was that they saw scriptural prophecy as having little to do with them because of its human authorship. The particularity of the people who wrote prophecy, due to their capacity to imagine their own ideas, stripped prophecy of any relevance it might have for Peter's opponents, though they no doubt saw that the prophecies were relevant to the prophets themselves. Like many contemporary readers of the Bible, the human aspect of the Scriptures acted as a barrier preventing them from being taken too seriously. Peter responds by asserting that both divine and human aspects of Scripture's genesis are fused. Prophets spoke because the Holy Spirit 'carried' them, enabling them to speak the very words of God. Because of the Holy Spirit, the obvious human element in the speaking and writing of Scripture does not distance Scripture from its readers, whether 800 or 2800 years after its first airing.

This understanding of the dual nature of Scripture provides the basis for furnishing biblical interpretation with appropriate distanciation. Scripture belongs to the past and should be understood in relation to its past, but, at the same time, it is not constrained by the past. It cannot be restrained because of its inspiration. The void which could be opened by historical difference is closed by God himself. Yet there remains another reason not to regard the passage of time as something which cuts contemporary readers off from authorially intended meanings of Scripture. Here we need to return to the use of Psalm 95 in Hebrews.

---

[82]   Bauckham, *Jude, 2 Peter*, p 235.

As was noted in the chapter on textual meaning, the author of Hebrews understands Psalm 95 to be both historical (originating on the lips of David) and current (introducing it with 'as the Holy Spirit *says*' in Hebrews 3:7 and applying it as a direct challenge to his audience). The historical text becomes direct discourse for the audience of Hebrews because of who they are. They are the house of God (3:6), God's people, analogous to God's people of the past. So the author of Hebrews can compare the Church in his day with the wilderness generation of God's people in the past in 4:2. Both groups had the Gospel preached to them; both groups faced the prospect of failing to enter into God's rest. At the same time, just as the words of Psalm 95 were a challenge to David's generation, residing in the land but not enjoying God's rest, so they offer the same challenge and promise to the Church. It is the identity of the readers of Psalm 95 as God's people that enables it to speak directly to them in Hebrews. The historical distance of the text is dissolved by the common identity of the 'them' to whom to text first spoke and the 'us' who read it in our own present. The original audience of Psalm 95 is not alien, as far as Christians are concerned, but are part of the same people of God with them. As the author of Hebrews makes clear in chapter 11 of his letter, the Church joins the people of God of the past in a common life of faith and a common pilgrimage to God's everlasting place of rest, his kingdom which cannot be shaken (Hebrews 12:28). As Murray A. Rae writes,

'The church is a body extended through space and time...The apostolic witness, therefore, for all that it has been shaped by the cultural conditions of the first century, is not something from which we are separated by a 'broad ugly ditch'. The apostles are not citizens of a world we no longer inhabit. They are part of the one community that is called into being and continues to be shaped by God to bear witness to the working out of his purpose. That christocentric and pneumatological reality overrides what differences there certainly are between Jew and Greek, male and female, ancient and modern, and thus enables the Spirit-inspired speech of the apostles to be heard 'in our own language.'[83]

Because God's people share a common history, a history which unites past and present, God's words of the past spoken for real human contexts by real human servants of God, can be read as addressing his people in the present. History is not a barrier to hearing and obeying God's voice in the Scriptures. Yet distanciation must be appropriate, taking into account the full complexity of the historical narrative in which God's promises are fulfilled. For example, to read God's promises of land to his people of the past, without any sense of how such promises have been fulfilled through the Lord Jesus, would be to make a grave mistake. Scripture is still historically contingent even though it can be read as being for us, now. God's eternal purpose is to create people for himself: a people who will bring glory to his holy name. This sovereign work is accomplished through history as a holy nation, descended from Abraham, is created, from the past, the present and the future: a people who will one day stand united in the new creation.

---

[83] As Murray A. Rae, 'Creation and Promise: Towards a Theology of History,' in *"Behind" the Text: History and Biblical Interpretation*, Ed., Craig Bartholomew, C. Stephen Evans, Mary Healy and Murray Rae (Paternoster/Zondervan: Carlisle/Michigan. 2003), p 296.

6.   Conclusion

Faithfully handling the word of truth is an awesome responsibility. Those entrusted with the privilege of teaching God's word should be aware that this activity provokes opposition simply by virtue of what it is. In 2 Timothy 3-4, where Paul urges Timothy to proclaim God's inspired word at all times, so much is made of the context in which biblical teaching will be heard. In fact, Paul's charge and explanation of what Scripture is and does is sandwiched between two accounts of the hostility those faithful to God and his word face. Objections to the way Evangelicals interpret the Bible will exist until the Lord returns. Sometimes these objections will be worth taking seriously. However, all the best explanations for our interpretations of Scripture will not take away the offensive nature of the Bible.

The aim of this study is to encourage the faithful interpretation of God's word by engaging with some of the questions raised against what Evangelicals might regard as best exegetical practice. Issues to do with biblical hermeneutics are likely to assume even greater importance than they already have in the great theological controversies of the 21st Century. At the same time, educated local people are most disposed to think of the interpretation of texts as a highly subjective enterprise. If we wish to proclaim the Bible's message of everlasting life through the Lord Jesus in our towns and in the global church, we need to be sure that what we say really is the Bible's message. We need to feel confident that it is in fact meaningful to talk about something called 'the message of Bible.' We need this confidence because it would be scandalous if the precious Gospel of the Lord Jesus, which so urgently needs to be heard by Christians and non-Christians alike, were proclaimed as an hypothesis: as a mere possibility, as simply one possible way of interpreting the Bible. The precious message of the Bible: God's redemption of his fallen creation through the saving death of God incarnate is such good news. It would be a scandal if this message were not proclaimed with the boldness it warrants.

LATIMER PUBLICATIONS

LATIMER PUBLICATIONS

LATIMER PUBLICATIONS

WTL	The Way, the Truth and the Life: Theological Resources for a Pilgrimage to a Global Anglican Future – eds. Vinay Samuel, Chris Sugden, Sarah Finch
AEID	Anglican Evangelical Identity – Yesterday and Today – J.I.Packer and N.T.Wright
IB	The Anglican Evangelical Doctrine of Infant Baptism – John Stott and J.Alec Motyer
BF	Being Faithful: The Shape of Historic Anglicanism Today – Theological Resource Group of GAFCON
FWC	The Faith we confess: An exposition of the 39 Articles – Gerald Bray
TPG	The True Profession of the Gospel: Augustus Toplady and Reclaiming our Reformed Foundations – Lee Gatiss
SG	Shadow Gospel: Rowan Williams and the Anglican Communion Crisis – Charles Raven
TTB	Translating the Bible: From Willliam Tyndale to King James – Gerald Bray
PWS	Pilgrims, Warriors, and Servants: Puritan Wisdom for Today's Church – ed. Lee Gatiss
PPA	Preachers, Pastors, and Ambassadors: Puritan Wisdom for Today's Church – ed. Lee Gatiss
CWP	The Church, Women Bishops and Provision: The Integrity of Orthodox Objections to the Proposed Legislation Allowing Women Bishops

Lightning Source UK Ltd.
Milton Keynes UK
UKOW052219131211

183686UK00001B/6/P